Quote Octopus
2/53 Barry Street,
Melbourne, Victoria, 3053
Australia
www.quoteoctopus.com

Dedication
This book is dedicated to the most die-hard fans of movies, directors, writers and every spirit that has captivated our imagination on the big screen.

Movies can and do have tremendous influence in shaping young lives in the realm of entertainment towards the ideals and objectives of normal adulthood.

Walt Disney

Pick up a camera. Shoot something. No matter how small, no matter how cheesy, no matter whether your friends and your sister star in it. Put your name on it as director. Now you're a director. Everything after that you're just negotiating your budget and your fee.

James Cameron

A film is - or should be - more like music than like fiction. It should be a progression of moods and feelings. The theme, what's behind the emotion, the meaning, all that comes later.

Stanley Kubrick

If you want a happy ending, that depends, of course, on where you stop your story.

Orson Welles

Everybody has something that chews them up and, for me, that thing was always loneliness. The cinema has the power to make you not feel lonely, even when you are.

Tom Hanks

The most amazing thing for me is that every single person who sees a movie, not necessarily one of my movies, brings a whole set of unique experiences. Now, through careful manipulation and good storytelling, you can get everybody to clap at the same time, to hopefully laugh at the same time, and to be afraid at the same time.

Steven Spielberg

When people ask me if I went to film school I tell them, 'no, I went to films.'

Quentin Tarantino

A story should have a beginning, a middle and an end, but not necessarily in that order.

Jean-Luc Godard

The length of a film should be directly related to the endurance of the human bladder.

Alfred Hitchcock

Filmmaking is a chance to live many lifetimes.

Robert Altman

Cinema should make you forget you are sitting in a theater.

Roman Polanski

A film is never really good unless the camera is an eye in the head of a poet.

Orson Welles

I made mistakes in drama. I thought drama was when actors cried. But drama is when the audience cries.

Frank Capra

The most honest form of filmmaking is to make a film for yourself.

Peter Jackson

Movies are like an expensive form of therapy for me.

Tim Burton

Movies are something people see all over the world because there is a certain need for it.

Wim Wenders

A good film is when the price of the dinner, the theatre admission and the babysitter were worth it.

Alfred Hitchcock

I think cinema, movies, and magic have always been closely associated. The very earliest people who made film were magicians.

Francis Ford Coppola

A cinema villain essentially needs a moustache so he can twiddle with it gleefully as he cooks up his next nasty plan.

Mel Brooks

The secret to film is that it's an illusion.

George Lucas

If my films make one more person miserable, I'll feel I have done my job.

Woody Allen

It's the movies that have really been running things in America ever since they were invented. They show you what to do, how to do it, when to do it, how to feel about it, and how to look how you feel about it.

Andy Warhol

I have a love interest in every one of my films: a gun.

Arnold Schwarzenegger

Learning to make films is very easy. Learning what to make films about is very hard.

George Lucas

Film lovers are sick people.

Francois Truffaut

A wide screen just makes a bad film twice as bad.

Samuel Goldwyn

Cinema is a matter of what's in the frame and what's out.

Martin Scorsese

Cinema is the most beautiful fraud in the world.

Jean-Luc Godard

You know what your problem is, it's that you haven't seen enough movies - all of life's riddles are answered in the movies.

Steve Martin

Acting is not about being famous, it's about exploring the human soul.

Annette Bening

Every great film should seem new every time you see it.

Roger Ebert

If you're sitting in your minivan, playing your computer animated films for your children in the back seat, is it the animation that's entertaining you as you drive and listen? No, it's the storytelling. That's why we put so much importance on story. No amount of great animation will save a bad story.

John Lasseter

The great art of films does not consist of descriptive movement of face and body but in the movements of thought and soul transmitted in a kind of intense isolation.

Louise Brooks

The difference between life and the movies is that a script has to make sense, and life doesn't.

Joseph L. Mankiewicz

I never thought I'd land in pictures with a face like mine.

Audrey Hepburn

Film spectators are quiet vampires.

Jim Morrison

To grasp the full significance of life is the actor's duty; to interpret it his problem; and to express it his dedication.

James Dean

Everything makes me nervous - except making films.

Elizabeth Taylor

There's only one thing that can kill the movies, and that's education.

Will Rogers

The movies are the only business where you can go out front and applaud yourself.

Will Rogers

If my films don't show a profit, I know I'm doing something right.

Woody Allen

A lot of movies are about life, mine are like a slice of cake.

Alfred Hitchcock

A film is a petrified fountain of thought.

Jean Cocteau

Give me a couple of years, and I'll make that actress an overnight success.

Samuel Goldwyn

When I was growing up, Dr. Seuss was really my favorite. There was something about the lyrical nature and the simplicity of his work that really hit me.

Tim Burton

I don't think you should feel about a film. You should feel about a woman, not a movie. You can't kiss a movie.

Jean-Luc Godard

Horror movies are the best date movies. There's no wondering , 'When do I put my arm around her?'

Eli Roth

I made over forty Westerns. I used to lie awake nights trying to think up new ways of getting on and off a horse.

William Wyler

The directing of a picture involves coming out of your individual loneliness and taking a controlling part in putting together a small world. A picture is made. You put a frame around it and move on. And one day you die. That is all there is to it.

John Huston

I'm not a huge fan of scary movies, but I love doing them because your character arc gets condensed, and everything is elevated, and so you kind of have this amazing opportunity to go in many different places.

Imogen Poots

I'm not a real movie star. I've still got the same wife I started out with twenty-eight years ago.

Will Rogers

I don't take the movies seriously, and anyone who does is in for a headache.

Bette Davis

A filmmaker has almost the same freedom as a novelist

has when he buys himself some paper.

Stanley Kubrick

Shoot a few scenes out of focus. I want to win the foreign film award.

Billy Wilder

If I can't get the girl, at least give me more money.

Alan Alda

Even if I set out to make a film about a fillet of sole, it would be about me.

Federico Fellini

The movies we love and admire are to some extent a function of who we are when we see them.

Mary Schmich

And I always had this idea for making a movie about a femme fatale, because I like these characters. They're a lot of fun, they're sexy, they're manipulative, they're dangerous.

Brian De Palma

A hit for me is if I enjoy the movie, if I personally enjoy the movie.

Ridley Scott

There's an electrical thing about movies.

Oliver Stone

So much of movie acting is in the lighting. And in loving your characters. I try to know them, and with that intimacy comes love. And now, I love Voldemort.

Ralph Fiennes

I think it would be very boring dramatically to have a film where everybody was a lawyer or doctor and had no faults. To me, the most important thing is to be truthful.

Spike Lee

I like the idea of movies having a magic element. How many times have you seen an actor in a movie who you know only as the character? It's wonderful, isn't it?

Christian Bale

I'm married to the theater but my mistress is the films.

Oskar Werner

Movies are not scripts - movies are films; they're not books, they're not the theatre.

Nicolas Roeg

Movies are a complicated collision of literature, theatre, music and all the visual arts.

Yahoo Serious

Movie magic is movie magic and acting magic is acting magic.

Ben Kingsley

The end of a picture is always an end of a life.

Sam Peckinpah

In the next couple of years, part of every film's process is going to be to adjust the images. And it'll be to change the color of an actor's tie or change the little smirky thing he's doing with his mouth. Or you can put in more clouds or move the tree a little bit.

Robert Zemeckis

You read a script and its based on 'Reservoir Dogs' and 'Pulp Fiction', and it goes right in the bin.

Tim Roth

I just like movies that somehow expose the world in a way that's different than you imagine it.

Alex Winter

I always loved silent movies. I was not a specialist, but I loved them. And when I started directing, I became really fascinated by the format - how it works, the device of the silent movie. It's not the same form of expression as a talkie. The lack of sounds makes you participate in the storytelling.

Michel Hazanavicius

You won't find me in a romantic comedy. Those movies don't speak to me. People don't come to talk to me about those scripts, because they probably think I'm this dark, twisted, miserable person.

Naomi Watts

The best reason to go to the movies is to be with other people. Eating the popcorn, being with other people you don't know.

Peter Weller

I do believe that movies are subject to a million interpretations.

Oliver Stone

Why should people go out and pay money to see bad films when they can stay at home and see bad television for nothing?

Samuel Goldwyn

Everyone told me to pass on 'Speed' because it was a 'bus movie.'

Sandra Bullock

I like something where I can really use my imagination and be an active participant in the construction of the monster and usually that's in the world of the supernatural or the world of the fantastic, so that's why those kinds of stories about demons and the supernatural appeal to me or maybe I'm really interested in that subject.

Sam Raimi

Every single art form is involved in film, in a way.

Sydney Pollack

I never enjoyed working in a film.

Marlene Dietrich

Most of us do not consciously look at movies.

Roger Ebert

Movies are like magic tricks.

Jeff Bridges

You can map your life through your favorite movies, and no two people's maps will be the same.

Mary Schmich

I didn't have any ambition to produce big mainstream popcorn movies.

Jodie Foster

I am a cynical optimist. Big opening weekends are like cotton candy. The films you will remember over time are the films that stick in the consciousness of the audience in a good way.

Robert Redford

I learned what I really love is making films, not the film business. I want to be on the set, meeting with writers, I want that freedom. I love it now.

Harvey Weinstein

Sometimes in movies, I still have to be the hero, but it's not all that important to me anymore.

Dennis Quaid

Filmmaking is a completely imperfect art form that takes years and, over those years, the movie tells you what it is.

Mistakes happen, accidents happen and true great films are the results of those mistakes and the decisions that those directors make during those moments.

Jason Reitman

Citizen Kane is perhaps the one American talking picture that seems as fresh now as the day it opened. It may seem even fresher.

Pauline Kael

People know that I have a great love for cinema. Not just for commercial cinema, but for the 'cinema d'auteur.' But to me, two of the great 'auteurs' are actually actors and they both happen to be French. One is Alain Delon and the other is Jean-Paul Belmondo.

Harvey Weinstein

And in movies you must be a gambler. To produce films is to gamble.

Douglas Sirk

It's the story that counts.

Vincente Minnelli

I make movies I want to see.

Neil LaBute

I was obsessed with romance. When I was in high school, I saw 'Doctor Zhivago' every day from the day it opened until the day it left the theater.

John Hughes

Every time I make a picture the critics' estimate of American public taste goes down ten percent.

Cecil B. DeMille

When you make a film you usually make a film about an idea.

Sydney Pollack

'Mr. Smith Goes to Washington' is one of the greatest films of all time.

Laura Dern

I think you kind of hope for people to gush over movies, but I think the opposite way is great sometimes, too. I'd rather have a movie that you're angry about and that you're talking about the next day, than something you forget about when the popcorn goes into the trash.

Gabriel Mann

I don't storyboard. I guess it dates back to my days in live television, where there was no possibility of storyboarding and everything was shot right on the spot - on the air, as we say - at the moment we were transmitting. I prefer to be open to what the actors do, how they interact to the given situation.

Arthur Penn

We are the movies and the movies are us.

David Ansen

So I like to try to go back and develop pure visual storytelling. Because to me, it's one of the most exciting aspects of making movies and almost a lost art at this point.

Brian De Palma

Everybody's a filmmaker today.

John Milius

If you don't like my movies, don't watch them.

Dario Argento

Hitchcock had a charm about him. He was very funny at times. He was incredibly brilliant in his field of suspense.

Tippi Hedren

I've made 122 movies, and I daresay there's a picture of mine showing somewhere in the world every day.

Tony Curtis

Movies are an art form that is very available to the masses.

Richard King

Well, the wonderful thing about making movies, oddly enough, is that they're sort of highly motivated graduate studies in one or another field.

Sydney Pollack

'Home Alone' was a movie, not an alibi.

Jerry Orbach

Nobody makes movies bad on purpose.

Roland Emmerich

Nothing to me is unexpected. No disappointment is
unexpected - whether it's movies or people or
relationships. I'm always ready for the punch directly
between the eyes. So I get hurt, but I never get hurt.
Happens all the time.

Brian Grazer

I wanted to escape Small Town U.S.A. To dismiss the
boundaries, to explore. My life experience came from
watching movies, TV, and reading books and magazines.
When your culture comes from watching TV everyday,
you're bombarded with images of things that seem cool,
places that seem interesting, people who have jobs and
careers and opportunities.

Trent Reznor

It is painful to watch children trying to show off for parents who are engrossed in their cell phones. Children are nostalgic for the 'good old days' when parents used to read to them without the cell phone by their side or watch football games or Disney movies without having the BlackBerry handy.

Sherry Turkle

Some mornings you wake up and think, gee I look handsome today. Other days I think, what am I doing in the movies? I wanna go back to Ireland and drive a forklift.

Liam Neeson

It'll be the Internet and piracy that will kill film. There's a philosophy that the Internet should be free, but the reality is that piracy will destroy the film industry and film as an art form because it's expensive to make a movie. Maybe you'll have funky little independent movies, and it'll go back and then start up again some other way.

Helen Mirren

I never was that boy who loved gangster films, but when I was growing up, I was obsessed with the detective Dick Tracy. It was one of my favourite movies as a kid, and he really inspired me. I would have loved to be part of that golden age of Hollywood in the 1940s. It made me want to become an actor.

Ryan Gosling

Sometimes over things that I did, movies that didn't turn out very well - you go, 'Why did you do that?' But in the end, I can't regret them because I met amazing people. There was always something that was worth it.

Robin Williams

To me, movies and music go hand in hand. When I'm writing a script, one of the first things I do is find the music I'm going to play for the opening sequence.

Quentin Tarantino

Some of my foster families used to send me to the movies to get me out of the house and there I'd sit all day and way into the night. Up in front, there with the screen so big, a little kid all alone, and I loved it. I loved anything that moved up there and I didn't miss anything that happened and there was no popcorn either.

Marilyn Monroe

Music is the only passion I shamelessly indulge in.

However, for recreation I enjoy watching movies. 'Wizard of Oz' was the first film I ever saw, followed by the 'Bond' movies. I also watch a lot of World cinema through DVDs mostly brought by one of my best friends who's now based in Toronto.

A. R. Rahman

Cancer taught me to stop saving things for a special occasion. Every day is special. You don't have to get cancer to start living life to the fullest. My post-cancer philosophy? No wasted time. No ugly clothes. No boring movies.

Regina Brett

I like to go out if there's a party or go to the movies, but I just like hanging out with my buddies and having a good time.

Jean-Luc Bilodeau

All my friends were in college when I was making 'Superbad.' We were drinking beer and watching movies and eating pizza. It wasn't like I was going to nice restaurants or anything like that, and I lived like a frat guy. Eventually it was time to grow up, be healthy and be responsible. You can't live like a kid forever, you know?

Jonah Hill

In the movies, you want a good story and characters that are honest, but you are also looking for a good director who can lead the ship. That's how we look at business. Everybody has a great idea for a start-up, and so do their relatives, and they tell me, 'You gotta build it.' I say, 'I have to believe in it.'

Ashton Kutcher

That's my fun time so, to me, doing my homework, studying on what I do, watching the movies, listening to music, all that inspires me so I focus a lot on that and practice.

Christina Milian

When I was a boy, I always saw myself as a hero in comic books and in movies. I grew up believing this dream.

Elvis Presley

I always hated high-school shows and high-school movies, because they were always about the cool kids. It was always about dating and sex, and all the popular kids, and the good-looking kids. And the nerds were super-nerdy cartoons, with tape on their glasses. I never saw 'my people' portrayed accurately.

Paul Feig

I was always raised on cowboy films, and then when I could start making choices about the movies I wanted to watch I found myself wanting to watch gangster films which were slightly more sophisticated than the baseline stuff that was in westerns.

Shia LaBeouf

I wanted to do another movie that could make us laugh and cry and feel good about the world. I wanted to do something else that could make us smile. This is a time when we need to smile more and Hollywood movies are supposed to do that for people in difficult times.

Steven Spielberg

There is evil prowling in the world - it shows up in our movies, video games and online fascinations, and finds its way into vulnerable hearts and minds.

Rick Perry

I don't want to do anything and everything. I want to be a brand that, every time I leverage my name, I want people to feel sure that it's going to be something good - so whether it be my movies, my perfume, my restaurant, my musical, it'll be good work, good food and good everything.

Shilpa Shetty

I remember saying goodbye to my father the night he left to join the Navy. He didn't have to. He was older than other servicemen and had a family to support but he wanted to be a part of the fight against fascism, not just make movies about it. I admired this about him.

Jane Fonda

Rap for me is like making movies, telling stories, and getting the emotions of the songs through in just as deep a way. And I grew up in rap and movies the same way.

Jay-Z

'Rosemary's Baby' is still one of my favorite movies of all time. The idea of her being impregnated with the devil is just so frightening. I'm actually going to work on a movie in February, called 'Mercy,' from Jason Blum, who produced the 'Paranormal Activity' movies, and there is a similar theme to 'Rosemary's Baby' in the movie.

Dylan McDermott

Life is more than sunglasses and hit movies. Reality - that's the main event.

Sylvester Stallone

I grew up when I was 15 when I had my first opportunity in movies. I watched every great movie for a year and a half, and since then I've asked myself how I can emulate such artistry. That's really my motivation. I want to do something as good as my heroes have done.

Leonardo DiCaprio

Man's inhumanity to man is as old as humanity itself. Some people just do evil things. Most do not. A billion people have seen 'Batman' movies over the past 20 years, and they have been entertained and inspired. One man saw it as a sick entry point for mass murder. The one is tragic. The billion are not. I choose to write for the billion.

Kurt Sutter

I had a couple of really cool friends when I was a kid, and we'd find cool music and movies and show them to each other. My friend Dennis had a copy of 'A Clockwork Orange' and he'd already seen it once, and he was like, 'We need to watch this.' I was sleeping over his house - and I think we were literally 15 - and we watched it.

Gerard Way

Our lives are pretty calm. Merging on the freeway in the closest you get to risking your life. So what's missing now is that primal emotion of being scared to death, and I think that's why people crave thrills like roller coasters or scary movies. They give you the chance to feel this very primal emotion in a very controlled environment.

Oren Peli

Hopefully, after 'Victorious' has lived a long and beautiful life, I would like to go into movies. And I'd like to have a very successful movie career. Ultimately I'd love to win an Oscar; that's my big goal in life, so that's what I'm going for.

Elizabeth Gillies

If you just love movies enough, you can make a good one.

Quentin Tarantino

As popular culture becomes more presentist, we move away from entertainment as the vicarious experience of a narrative - as watching someone else's story - and much more toward enacting one's own story. Moving away from myths and toward fantasy role-playing games, away from movies and toward videogames.

Douglas Rushkoff

I never expected anyone to take care of me, but in my wildest dreams and juvenile yearnings, I wanted the house with the picket fence from June Allyson movies. I knew that was yearning like one yearns to fly.

Maya Angelou

I'm definitely a romantic comedy dude because I'm a big romantic at heart. I'm a softy, so it's always nice to watch movies that make you think that love at first sight is actually possible.

Sterling Knight

The elements that create glamour are not specific styles - bias-cut gowns or lacquered furniture - but more general qualities: grace, mystery, transcendence. To the right audience, Halle Berry is more glamorous commanding the elements as Storm in the X-Men movies than she is walking the red carpet in a designer gown.

Virginia Postrel

The movies were so healing for me because I had such an isolated, lonely childhood. Going to the movies and having the lights go down, you disappear. If you have esteem issues, suddenly you're in a void where nobody can see you. You are just by yourself in that darkness, and your loneliness is cured.

Michael De Luca

I never think it's right to chew gum in front of other people, but a lot of times I'll come in for a meeting chewing gum and I'll forget I'm chewing it. Then you don't want to swallow it because it stays in your system for seven years or something, so I've asked to throw it away. I've started to wonder if that's why I didn't get certain movies.

Jennifer Lawrence

Everything I learned I learned from the movies.

Audrey Hepburn

With the CGI, suddenly there's a thousand enemies instead of six - the army goes off into the horizon. You don't need that. The audience loses its relationship with the threat on the screen. That's something that's consistently happening and it makes these movies like video games and that's a soulless enterprise. It's all kinetics without emotion.

Harrison Ford

I've done movies with Oliver Stone and Michael Mann. And I've done quite a few dramas in my time, from the theatre to film work. I just think the audience is used to seeing me on 'Saturday Night Live,' and 'K-9,' and 'Curly Sue' and of course, 'According to Jim.' I think that my comedies have been the most popular.

James Belushi

Nobody should come to the movies unless he believes in heroes.

John Wayne

Whatever happened to books? Suddenly everybody's talking about these 100-hour movies called 'Breaking Bad'. People are talking about TV the same way they used to talk about novels back in the 1980s. I like to think I hang out with some pretty smart people, but all they talk about is 'Breaking Bad.'

Douglas Coupland

In Hollywood, they think drawn animation doesn't work anymore, computers are the way. They forget that the reason computers are the way is that Pixar makes good movies. So everybody tries to copy Pixar. They're relying too much on the technology and not enough on the artists.

Tim Burton

Football games are on TV, and it doesn't affect stadium attendance at all. It's the same with movies. People who really love movies and like to go out on a Saturday night will go to the movie theater.

George Lucas

Movies can't ruin books. They can only ruin movies.

S. E. Hinton

Movies always are open to being remade because times change so much, and the tempo of movies changes. I think of it like a James Bond. They can have different actors play the same role... I've had people come up to me and say, 'We want to remake 'The Jerk' with so and so.' And I say, 'Fine.' It just doesn't bother me. It's an honor actually.

Steve Martin

I was dirt-poor. I could barely hold down a job. Eventually, though, I started getting small parts on shows like 'Smallville,' 'Supernatural'... and lots of really bad sci-fi movies. I was running around the woods in wolf contacts, covered in fake blood made out of pancake syrup, roaring.

Cory Monteith

It's a great feeling to think that I can be a friend to so many people through my movies.

River Phoenix

There's this little box that African-American actors have to work in, in the first place, and I was able to rise above that box. I could have done a bunch of movies where I stayed as the Axel Foley or Reggie Hammond persona. But I didn't want to be doing the same thing all the time. Every now and then, you crash and burn, but that's part of it.

Eddie Murphy

I find 'Edward Scissorhands' a very inspiring movie - it's one of the first movies about bullying, in a way - about being treated unkindly for being different.

Denise Di Novi

I don't want to be in somebody else's movie, and then they make all the money. I've gotten offers to do the movies, but I won't sell myself short and be in somebody else's movie, like 'Boyz N the Hood.' I don't think I woulda done that.

Eazy-E

Those movies sure got me into a rut.

Elvis Presley

Even in India the Hindi film industry might be the best known but there are movies made in other regional languages in India, be it Tamil or Bengali. Those experiences too are different from the ones in Bombay.

Aishwarya Rai Bachchan

I grew up on certain movies, particular movies that said something to me as a kid from Missouri, movies that showed me places I'd yet traveled, or different cultures, or explained something, or said something in a better way than I could ever say. I wanted to find the movies like that.

Brad Pitt

I'm not a big fan of kids' movies that have this knowing snarkiness to them or this post-modern take on storytelling. I think that sails right over the heads of most kids. There's something to be said for a well-told fairy tale. There's a reason that these mythic stories stay with us.

John C. Reilly

We need to see men and women as equal partners, but it's hard to think of movies that do that. When I talk to people, they think of movies of forty-five years ago! Hepburn and Tracy!

Betty Friedan

It's time for me to do things I like so I will be happy, my wife will be happy, my friends will be happy. I just want to do something I'm proud of. It's time for me to change. I could sign with a company for 10 movies and I'm the king of video and so what?

Jean-Claude Van Damme

I do enjoy animated movies. I really love anime and movies like 'Spirited Away' and 'Howl's Moving Castle.'

Nicolas Cage

In life, single women are the most vulnerable adults. In movies, they are given imaginary power.

Elizabeth Wurtzel

I've always been a movie guy, movies have been my thing.
I love movies, all kinds of movies.

Christopher Nolan

In most movies there is a Prince Charming who rides up
and saves the girl.

Zoe Lister-Jones

I'm going to do all my movies here in Chicago. The
'Tribune' referred to me as a 'former Chicagoan.' As if, to
do anything, I had to leave Chicago. I never left. I worked
until I was 29 at the Leo Burnett advertising agency, and
then I quit to do this. This is a working city, where people
go to their jobs and raise their kids and live their lives.

John Hughes

It can have an enormous effect because big budget movies
can have big budget perks, and small budget movies have
no perks, but what is the driving force, of course, is the
script, and your part in it.

Morgan Freeman

I don't know many women who can relate to Sharon Stone and the kind of movies she does. I don't know a lot of guys who can relate to Tom Cruise's movies because they're on a kind of fantastic level.

Kim Cattrall

'Seanan McGuire' is my real name; if I'm being silly and third-person about it, she's a frequently cranky, foul-mouthed Disney Princess on vacation in the real world, where she studies diseases, cuddles reptiles, watches lots of horror movies, and goes to as many corn fields as possible.

Seanan McGuire

The irony is that the more unapologetically sexist men are in movies, the more women tend to be attracted to them in person.

Jon Favreau

You go through this business and you meet people that you bond with, and you get to go make movies with them. It's wonderful. What I've always dreamt of, in my career, is to have a brotherhood of collaborators, and go in and out of working with them. I'm just starting to get that, and it's really lovely.

Charlie Hunnam

I enjoy the old-fashioned idea of, like, 'His Girl Friday' and 'Bringing Up Baby', those old movies.

Judy Greer

When I made 'Real Steel,' the director actually had the robots in the monitor, so he knew where everything was. So technically, there's been advancements. But at the end of the day, movies are about story and characters, so all the other stuff is great, but unless you have those two elements, then you've got nothing.

Hugh Jackman

When videotape came so a lot of movies that I do have a kind of afterlife in video. Things where movies that I do would come and go; they still come and go but you can go rent them and see them on TV.

Christopher Walken

I love horror, I love scary movies, I love thrillers. If things creep you out and spook you? I love it.

Lana Parrilla

A lot of movies about artificial intelligence envision that AI's will be very intelligent but missing some key emotional qualities of humans and therefore turn out to be very dangerous.

Ray Kurzweil

I've always wanted to get into acting, ever since I was younger. I'd put on shows for my family and run around play dress-up all the time. I think I was 4 when I told them I wanted to do movies.

Emma Roberts

It took me 20 years of making movies to learn how to do it.

Chevy Chase

It's difficult to do a genre film well, and it doesn't matter if you're talking vampire movies or 'Dawn of the Dead' or 'The Thing' or 'Escape From New York.' Those kind of movies, they understand what the old-school B-movie is supposed to be, they get the throwback of it.

Ethan Hawke

Any girl who likes watching movies would like to work in them and would want to do all of that. I'm also one of them. But people know me for badminton and love me for it. So I'd stick to it right now. But maybe after badminton, I'll think about it.

Saina Nehwal

I guess I can't live without Netflix because I would have nothing to do. All I do is sit home and watch movies.

Sara Paxton

I think you get less takes on TV than in movies.

Evan Peters

I like to be someone else. I like to be someone other than myself. I grew up watching movies and being a fan of what I'd seen portrayed in the movies, and I always wanted to do that one day.

Quinton Aaron

I always wish the hotels were like they are in movies and TV shows, where if you're in Paris, right outside your window is the Eiffel Tower. In Egypt, the pyramids are right there. In the movies, every hotel has a monument right outside your window. My hotel rooms overlook the garbage dumpster in the back alley.

Gilbert Gottfried

Jesus is a half-naked guy, hanging, nailed to a cross, and then people wear that around their neck, and then those are the people that are upset about violence in movies.

Marilyn Manson

I grew up thinking that I would become a fighter pilot and was fascinated by aircrafts as I had grown up around that. But my father encouraged me to not become an Air Force person, given the varied interests I had, be it books, movies, sports or fighter flying.

Kapil Sharma

I couldn't be happier about being a part of 'Hunger Games' and to play Katniss. I have a huge responsibility to the fans of this incredible book and I don't take it lightly. I will give everything I have to these movies and to this role to make it worthy of Suzanne Collins' masterpiece.

Jennifer Lawrence

I don't want to criticize any other designers, but I have to say that many of the people involved in this industry - directors and producers - are trying to make their games more like movies. They are longing to make movies rather than making videogames.

Shigeru Miyamoto

I used to look at horror movies as being really real and it would totally freak me out and give me nightmares. Now I watch and think, 'whoa how'd they do that?'

Evan Peters

I did four movies where I gained, like, fifty pounds. I had curly hair, and I had all of this facial hair. I had put on all this weight for these movies, and I did four or five of them back-to-back. Then I cut the weight and I got fit again. I cut my beard and I took away the mustache, and people were like, 'What are you doing?'

A. J. Bowen

I never really got nightmares from movies. In fact, I recall my father saying when I was three years old that I would be scared, but I never was. I was much more terrified by my own family and real life, you know?

Tim Burton

I like old movies, screwball comedies, vintage clothes, and basically I'm an old-fashioned gal.

Zooey Deschanel

At the heart of every really good Christmas movie is the threat, I suppose, to Christmas. Something is wrong with Christmas, in all of these movies. In 'The Polar Express,' there's a kid that doesn't really believe, and that's the threat to Christmas. In 'Santa Claus: The Movie,' jealousy and greed are threatening to overrun his Christmas.

James McAvoy

Right now I just want to chill for a while. Take a hiatus from all the craziness. To clean my house, see my family. Just see some movies and pick some strawberries.

Lauren Ambrose

I realized this is what God has dealt me, and I should be thankful considering all that's happened to me in my life, but MS caused the movies to stop - stop dead - and I miss it.

Richard Pryor

Not that it entirely matters: There is a perception that all actors make their movies. A lot of people assume you're responsible. George Clooney told me actors get all of the blame and all the credit.

Ben Affleck

In Malaysia, where Western culture was extremely influential, I'd grown up listening to Elvis and the Beatles and watching American movies. People wanted to be like Americans. In contrast, when I got here, I saw prosperous middle-class American college students wanting to somehow join the Third World.

Feisal Abdul Rauf

I think violence, cynicism, brutality and fashion are the staples of our diet. I think in the grand history of story-telling, going back to people sitting around fires, the dark side of human nature has always been very important. Movies are part of that tradition.

Eric Stoltz

Life is short. I'm 47 years old. I've got 10 years to go where I can be the best I can be. I want those 10 years to be precious, not like before, cranking two or three movies a year. I've made a ton of movies in my life, but so what?

Jean-Claude Van Damme

Becoming emancipated at 14, my life wasn't normal. I didn't have to go to school, so I didn't. I was rebellious by nature. I spent my 20s focusing on my company, Flower Films, and producing movies. Now that I'm almost 30, I would like to try other things in lie. I'm crazy about photography, and I want to take an art history class.

Drew Barrymore

Movies are my religion and God is my patron. I'm lucky enough to be in the position where I don't make movies to pay for my pool. When I make a movie, I want it to be everything to me; like I would die for it.

Quentin Tarantino

There's always room out there for the hand-drawn image. I personally like the imperfection of hand drawing as opposed to the slick look of computer animation. But you can do good stuff either way. The Pixar movies are amazing in what they do, but there's plenty of independent animators who are doing really amazing things as well.

Matt Groening

Whenever I have free time, I love to just lay in my bed and

watch YouTube videos, watch movies. Just basically do nothing.

Bethany Mota

I wish that my life could be like the movies, like 'Bonnie and Clyde' or 'The Hunger' or 'Harold and Maude.' And... it can be! It maybe just takes somebody else who is as fearless as you. It takes a person who will not hesitate.

Marilyn Manson

Adding sound to movies would be like putting lipstick on the Venus de Milo.

Mary Pickford

Cell phones tend to bring us more inside of our lives whereas movies offer a chance to escape, so there are two competing forces.

Steven Spielberg

My bar for being successful is being able to do movies that really mean something to me and being able to make a living off of that.

Channing Tatum

My movies just kind of sneak up on you. I don't have to worry too much about what everybody is going to say. Anyway, I really don't pay attention to what the world says about my movies. I just care about what my buddies think.

Adam Sandler

I was kind of a dark kid. I loved Halloween, and I loved vampires and the black and white old monster movies.

Joe Manganiello

I make movies for teenage boys. Oh dear, what a crime.

Michael Bay

My favorite thing of all time is a New York City weekend when there's a blizzard. Everything gets really quiet, and everyone goes to the movies and the park.

Idina Menzel

My favorite movies are movies that I go in and I leave deeply affected. Whether I laugh really hard or whether I cry really hard, I just want to feel really affected in that moment.

Shailene Woodley

Where I came from, just nodding and smiling when someone expressed views was the ultimate insult. If people weren't yelling about politics in our house then they were arguing about music, or movies, or food.

Ezekiel Emanuel

When we go to see comedians or funny movies, they don't address the wall behind them; they face us. This is why a game's first job is to entertain through gameplay and secondarily through humor, drama, or other traditional entertainment devices. The humor has to be a gentleman. I mean, it needs to be squeezed in around the game.

Doug TenNapel

Since I am from Spain, once the morning has gone, I like to take a nap while falling asleep to black and white movies. It feels less lonely. There is a comfort in hearing their voices, like when you're a child and your mother tells you a story before bedtime.

Jordi Molla

I think they should have movies in restaurants. I can't believe that so many people get together just to sit there.

It's so abstract... isn't it abstract? What are these people
sitting here watching?

Andy Warhol

The whole world loves American movies, blue jeans, jazz
and rock and roll. It is probably a better way to get to
know our country than by what politicians or airline
commercials represent.

Billy Joel

I don't like comedy. I like funny things. I don't like
comedy. Like, comedy movies are just, 'Oh Jesus.'

Louis C. K.

I've been to two festivals in my life, and I've never been to
Toronto. I haven't really been making festival movies. This
is new territory for me.

Joss Whedon

My dream role would probably be a psycho killer, because
the whole thing I love about movies is that you get to do
things you could never do in real life, and that would be
my way of vicariously experiencing being a psycho killer.
Also, it's incredibly romantic.

Christina Ricci

I do like escapism. I like going to the movies on a Friday night and seeing something fun.

Charlie Kaufman

I was going to go to a four-year college and be an anthropologist or to an art school and be an illustrator when a friend convinced me to learn photography at the University of Southern California. Little did I know it was a school that taught you how to make movies! It had never occurred to me that I'd ever have any interest in filmmaking.

George Lucas

As an actor, I'm attracted to drama; as a director, it's humor - because it's the story of my life, and I can't be that serious about it. Being alone is a big theme in all my movies, both as a director and as an actress.

Jodie Foster

I'm not impressed by someone's degree... I'm impressed by them making movies.

Richard King

I just grew up watching a lot of movies. I'm attracted to this genre and that genre, this type of story, and that type of story. As I watch movies I make some version of it in my head that isn't quite what I'm seeing - taking the things I like and mixing them with stuff I've never seen before.

Quentin Tarantino

I don't know that much about who directs what movies, but I'm definitely inspired by the look of old movies; I find them to be really beautiful.

Lana Del Rey

Oh, I adored Mickey Mouse when I was a child. He was the emblem of happiness and funniness. You went to the movies then, you saw two movies and a short. When Mickey Mouse came on the screen and there was his big head, my sister said she had to hold onto me. I went berserk.

Maurice Sendak

'Sunset Boulevard' - the story of Hollywood movies draped on a depressing sex affair - is an uncompromising study of American decadence displaying a sad, worn, methodical beauty few films have had since the late twenties.

Manny Farber

I hate movies that tell people what to think. I'm proud that Democrats thought 'Thank You For Smoking' was their film and Republicans thought it was theirs. I'm proud that pro-choice people thought 'Juno' was their film and pro-life people thought it was theirs.

Jason Reitman

I met Will Smith twice. I didn't talk to him for too long but I was trying to let him know that my age group grew up watching him - he was the coolest guy on television and the coolest guy in movies.

J. Cole

The classic war movies of the post-Vietnam era have generally taken on grand, philosophical themes: the meaninglessness of war, the grinding down of man by the machine - the machine being war itself, represented by someone like Gunnery Sergeant Hartman in 'Full Metal Jacket,' the sadistic marine who turns his boys into instruments of death.

Hanna Rosin

Well, the thing about great fictional characters from

literature, and the reason that they're constantly turned into characters in movies, is that they completely speak to what makes people human.

Keira Knightley

In old movies, the cinematography is a thousand times better than anything today. Writing, a thousand times better.

John Kricfalusi

I only make movies to finance my fishing.

Lee Marvin

When I was little I used to dance and model and that was fun. But I was always the person that was goofing off and I would memorize every line in every movie that I saw. And at recess that's what I would do, I would talk to my friends and recite movies.

Ashley Benson

I don't want to be a part of the demographics. I want to be an individual. I wear each of my films as a badge of pride. That's why I cherish all my bad reviews. If the critics start liking my movies, then I'm in deep trouble.

John Carpenter

There are lots of people with mental health disabilities, and that's just the way their life is; it's not like you see it in the movies.

Andy Behrman

I go to movies, go out with friends, go to car shows. I have a zoo.

Axl Rose

I'm an actor. And I guess I've done so many movies I've achieved some high visibility. But a star? I guess I still think of myself as kind of a worker ant.

Forest Whitaker

My folks always let me go to the movies every Saturday. We were really motion-picture goers.

John Wayne

I've never understood the cult of Hitchcock. Particularly the late American movies... Egotism and laziness. And they're all lit like television shows.

Orson Welles

People sometimes say the way things happen in the movies is unreal, but actually, it's the way things happen to you in life that's unreal.

Andy Warhol

I like zombie movies. I like 'The Walking Dead;' I like the metaphor of it, simply because when we go with the zombie concept - if you're bitten by a zombie, you don't transform into something else like a vampire or a werewolf or whatever. You become something that's not you.

Marilyn Manson

The next thing I knew, I was out of the service and making movies again. My first picture was called, GI Blues. I thought I was still in the army.

Elvis Presley

You take somebody that cries their goddam eyes out over phoney stuff in the movies, and nine times out of ten they're mean bastards at heart.

J. D. Salinger

I sure lost my musical direction in Hollywood. My songs were the same conveyer belt mass production, just like most of my movies were.

Elvis Presley

In the movies, I kill guys with an axe. In real life, I can't control a nine-year-old girl.

Sylvester Stallone

Later on they send me to Hollywood. To make movies. It was all new to me. I was only 21 years old.

Elvis Presley

America had, for one thing, lived in anarchy for - until much more recently than Europe. We had the Wild West, where the cliche of the cowboy movies was the nearest sheriff is 90 miles away, and so you had to pack a gun and defend yourself.

Steven Pinker

We can now have action movies with two stars where one might be African American and one might be Asian

American. One of them doesn't have to be white, and the other one doesn't have to be the ethnic sidekick. We're way over that. And I think it's happening in society, too.

Roger Ebert

I'm an enormous admirer of Christopher Lee. He's somebody, along with Vincent Price, who I celebrate, and I wanted my movies to show that celebration and that honoring of these great film stars that were unafraid to go into horror and Grand Guignol and the macabre.

Nicolas Cage

'Knowing' is one of those movies where you're going to get the spectacle, and you're going to have the entertainment in the grand science fiction tradition. But also, it will perhaps stimulate some discussion to help you sort out on your own where you might choose to go in terms of your own needs. Now, I say that without preaching.

Nicolas Cage

There were two movies that asked me to go to Australia or New Zealand for long periods of time. One was 'Lord of the Rings' and one was 'The Matrix.' But I was actively involved at that time raising my family, and I couldn't really take that time out.

Nicolas Cage

I always loved all kinds of music. I would watch musicals a lot as a kid, on TV, watch the Fred Astaire movies. I'd watch 'The Wizard of Oz.' I was a big Jerry Lewis fan, and they'd have these big bands and someone singing - some siren, or some guy singing some gorgeous song. I was always enamored of that style of music.

Queen Latifah

The nature of the movies is different than it was five years ago, and they're all driven by the possibilities of CGI, which means you can make anything happen on screen that you can possibly desire.

Tom Hanks

To me, the scariest movie ever made to this day is 'The Exorcist.' It still scares the living hell out of me, and it's because of the fantasy element. It's the exorcism. It's the Devil. It's not a guy breaking into your house trying to torture you or cut your whatever off. Those kinds of movies don't do it for me, and I don't call them horror.

Cassandra Peterson

I want to be like Tom Cruise from 'The Outsiders' and go

on and do amazing movies for a long time.

Ashton Kutcher

Sexiness, particularly in movies, is the chess game in the 'Thomas Crown Affair'. It's, it's, I don't know, but Faye Dunaway comes up a lot in that thinking. It's the subtlety of sexiness. The moment you try to be sexy, then it's not.

Daniel Craig

If there's specific resistance to women making movies, I just choose to ignore that as an obstacle for two reasons: I can't change my gender, and I refuse to stop making movies.

Kathryn Bigelow

I am really proud that I am one of the artists that has the opportunity to be on magazine covers and to be in the movies.

Beyonce Knowles

One of the nice things about books as opposed to television and movies to some extent is it's not a passive entertainment. People really do get involved, and they do create, and they do have their own visions of what different characters look like and what should happen. It's great - it means their brains are working.

James Patterson

What I fell in love with as a child was 'My Fair Lady,' 'Funny Face,' 'American in Paris,' and 'Singin' in the Rain.' Just perfect movies to me and I was dancing. I started ballet when I was three. And I fell in love with those movies and fell in love with Audrey Hepburn and Leslie Caron.

Dianna Agron

Any time you stop looking at evil as a black and white thing, it's helpful. So the fact that there won't be any obligatory Islamic terrorist stereotypes in movies any more, that'd be helpful.

John Cusack

People don't learn science in movies. You don't go to the movies thinking, 'I hope I learn some quantum mechanics this afternoon.' But on the other hand, movies are instrumental and influential in getting young people interested in science.

Seth Shostak

I'm fed up with the idiots... the ever-widening gap between people who know how to make movies and the people who green-light the movies.

Sean Connery

There's nothing more important in making movies than the screenplay.

Richard Attenborough

I don't want to imitate life in movies; I want to represent it. And in that representation, you use the colors you feel, and sometimes they are fake colors. But always it's to show one emotion.

Pedro Almodovar

Not everybody goes to movies to get their life changed.

Samuel L. Jackson

I'm into 'The Walking Dead,' 'Shaun of the Dead,' obviously, and I've seen all the Romero movies. I am a classic zombie queen. And I love the White Walkers on 'Game of Thrones.' Weirdly, it wasn't until pretty late in life that I found my entry point into horror films.

Anna Kendrick

I just want to sing, I want to work on my music, I want to make my movies, that's all I want to do.

Marc Anthony

Dr. Kissinger was a former child. Jerry Ford was a former child. Even F.D.R. was a former child. I retired from the movies in 1949, and I'm still a former child.

Shirley Temple

It's very difficult to judge yourself. Extreme self-doubt is only attractive when it's fictionalized. Which is why people love the movies. They are so reassuring.

Claire Danes

I think movies are great and I have a great time making them but they're not what keeps you warm at night, or what's ultimately the most important thing in anyone's life journey.

Reese Witherspoon

Scientists appear most often in horror movies. Through

childlike curiosity or God-defying hubris, they unleash destructive forces they can't control - 'Forbidden Planet''s Monsters of the Id.

Virginia Postrel

All through my life what I've loved doing is watching movies. I love the escapism of film, I love stories. So it is incredible to be able to be in them as much as I am, to see them from the first stitch in a costume to the end product.

Keira Knightley

I like movies where you can come back and re-watch them and admire the cinematography 25 years later.

Rob Zombie

Sometimes we see the Civil War in movies and imagine these neatly aligned rows of men with muskets, walking in line to shoot each other. In reality the things that fascinated me were how absolutely ruthless and violent so many engagements were, how much suffering and how men were not prepared.

Seth Grahame-Smith

Watching movies in the U.S. is great fun because they get

every joke, they smile, they laugh so much; it's a great feeling.

Jet Li

Just because you've made a couple movies, you've done some good movies, you've been nominated for some Academy Awards, whatever, nobody's entitled. It's a business. If they don't see it, I can think they're wrong, but I'm not entitled to a $15 million budget to make a film.

Edward Norton

People wrestle sometimes making movies, and I think that conflict is a very essential thing. I think a lot of very happy productions have produced a lot of very banal movies.

Edward Norton

What do I geek out about? What am I? Hmmm. I love movies. I watch movies. I like big, sweeping epics, like Ed Zwick stuff: 'The Last Samurai,' 'Legends of the Fall,' 'Blood Diamond,' 'Glory.'

Chris Evans

I've done movies I'm very proud of, but there's always a sense of: 'Come see this shiny new car!' The question I hate the most is: 'Why should people see it?'

Oscar Isaac

I'm relaxed about my career. I've been making movies for over 20 years, so I've earned at least the right to relax.

Eddie Murphy

Two things in India are religion - one is cricket, and one is movies - these are two things.

Preity Zinta

I really don't like to do back-to-back movies. I concentrate on things at home. My family and school life are important to me. I try to do one movie a year.

Anna Chlumsky

I'm not a big prank guy, because I don't like them done to me. I've been on movies sets where one guys goes into his trailer, and then people move the stairs, and he comes out of his trailer, and there's no stairs. That's not funny! I don't want to be that guy!

Terry Crews

It's a required part of your film history to know who Woody is. His movies are so wonderful, and not just funny but so insightful about human behavior.

Scarlett Johansson

I love beautiful black-and-white movies - anything Bette Davis, especially 'Now', 'Voyager', 'Casablanca', 'Mildred Pierce'; anything by Orson Welles, Truffaut, or Godard; and 'Paper Moon' by Peter Bogdanovich.

Suzan-Lori Parks

Born of the impossibly varied options we have to amuse ourselves, cutting-edge companies are finding innovative ways to tailor our entertainment choices to who we are, relieving us of the burden of finding the diamond in the rough of 500 TV channels or thousands of movies and music albums released every year.

Marcus Buckingham

I like to look like a person. It drives me crazy when you see women in movies playing teachers, and they have biceps. It totally takes me out of the movie. I start thinking, Wow, that actress playing this part really looks great!

Emma Stone

Critics can say what they like about the films, but very often, there's a certain expectation of documentaries that they're supposed to be like PowerPoint presentations. I see documentaries as movies. So when I see some critics writing that we could have done without the recreations altogether - well, perhaps.

Alex Gibney

I'm not allowed to see R-rated movies, but I did see 'Kick-Ass' because I'm in it. I'm not going to skip out on my own premiere!

Chloe Grace Moretz

The first fashion show I ever attended was for Ritu Beri in 1997 or 1998. I think that was the first time Ritu had designed for one of my movies 'Yeh Raastein Hain Pyaar Ke.' She had done a show in Paris, and she had done the same show in Delhi. It was very eclectic, and I love the way she combines colours and makes them flamboyant.

Madhuri Dixit

I can't say I was like a die-hard zombie fan, but I've definitely seen a few different zombie movies and TV shows.

Dave Franco

I'd skip school regularly to see movies - even in the morning, in the small Parisian theaters that opened early.

Francois Truffaut

If I can sell out clubs and theaters and play dirtbags in movies, and get blown up in a car or get the crap beat out of me in a movie, that's good for me; I'm good.

Bill Burr

I'll watch movies I like to see, Steve Jobs interviews, something that's going to make me smart and then go to sleep.

Jaden Smith

Usually you're in movies with a lot of dissolves and things, but this was kind of quick, more jarring than usual. I thought it would be fun to be in a movie that's unconventional. Then I met Guy and I liked him. I think he's a good man.

Dennis Farina

I really detest movies like 'Indecent Proposal' and 'Pretty

Woman' because they send a message to women that sleeping with a rich man is the ultimate goal and really that's such a small part of it.

Laura Kightlinger

The thing about HD-DVD that is attractive to Microsoft is that it's very pro-consumer in letting you copy all movies up onto the hard disk.

Bill Gates

I think with movies I am really connecting to the Joseph Campbell idea of the collective unconscious.

Will Smith

My skin is hard when it comes to my music. But with my movies, I'm still a virgin in a lot of ways. I'm not used to being shot down for no reason.

Will Smith

Over the years all these vampire movies have come out and nobody looks like a vampire anymore.

Johnny Depp

Acting and the industry of making movies is beautiful, but it's so exhausting and such hard work; if you don't absolutely 100% want to do something, it defeats the purpose.

Debby Ryan

Movies are a fad. Audiences really want to see live actors on a stage.

Charlie Chaplin

I think I made essential a mistake in staying in movies, because I - but it's a mistake I can't regret, because it's like saying, 'I shouldn't have stayed married to that woman, but I did because I love her.'

Orson Welles

One of my movies was called 'True Lies.' It's what the Democrats should have called their convention.

Arnold Schwarzenegger

I was striving to be the most muscular man, and it got me into the movies. It got me everything that I have.

Arnold Schwarzenegger

So, one way or another, I found myself in a few movies. I take it seriously when I'm on the set, but I don't take myself seriously as an actor.

Henry Rollins

There's a lot of great movies that have won the Academy Award, and a lot of great movies that haven't. You just do the best you can.

Clint Eastwood

Advertising is a racket, like the movies and the brokerage business. You cannot be honest without admitting that its constructive contribution to humanity is exactly minus zero.

F. Scott Fitzgerald

I like Italian movies. I was frequently there in the '60s, in Rome and the vicinity. It was a great period in life. I was very influenced by their stuff.

Clint Eastwood

Sometimes music, movies and books are the only things

that let us feel like someone else feels like we do.

Marilyn Manson

Minimalism seems closest to the sophisticated storytelling of movies. Movies have really educated contemporary audiences to be the most intelligent, sophisticated audiences in history. We don't any longer need to have the relationship between one scene and the next explained. We will figure it out ourselves.

Chuck Palahniuk

Watching movies is my one distraction.

Marilyn Manson

A big reason why I started writing is I felt that fiction had stopped evolving. All other entertainments were getting better, constantly, as technology allowed. Movies. Video games. Music.

Chuck Palahniuk

I love the movies, and when I go to see a movie that's been made from one of my books, I know that it isn't going to be exactly like my novel because a lot of other people have interpreted it. But I also know it has an idea that I'll like because that idea occurred to me, and I spent a year, or a year and a half of my life working on it.

Stephen King

Of the big horror movies of the '70s, you have 'The Omen,' 'The Sentinel,' 'Rosemary's Baby,' 'The Stepford Wives,' 'Burnt Offerings' - these are all romantic fatalist movies where there's a sort of glimmer of hope... but darkness wins.

Chuck Palahniuk

The folks who read my books are so passionate about each one of them that the people making my movies are more afraid of my readership than they are of me.

Chuck Palahniuk

My favorite movies of all times is 'Doctor Zhivago,' and I love 'Gone With the Wind.' I'd love to play some Southern belle or something where I owned a plantation.

Dolly Parton

Now on Friday nights, if I want to go hang out with friends, I go hang out with friends. If I want to stay in and be in the hot tub and have people over to watch movies, I do that.

Demi Lovato

Too much TV hurts movies.

Elvis Presley

I think less is more when it comes to kissing in the movies.

Julia Roberts

There are a lot of movies that are unbelievable successes that I would be mortified to be a part of.

Jennifer Aniston

I have been pregnant in so many movies it's ridiculous.

Jennifer Aniston

Making movies is not rocket science. It's about relationships and communication and strangers coming together to see if they can get along harmoniously, productively, and creatively. That's a challenge. When it works, it's fantastic and will lift you up. When it doesn't work, it's almost just as fascinating.

Julia Roberts

Somebody asked me about the current choice we're being given in the presidential election. I said, Well, it's like two of the scariest movies I can imagine.

Dean Koontz

You know you've been around when they start to remake your own movies when you're still alive.

Sylvester Stallone

Right now, my job is that I'm like an ambulance chaser. I've got to look for movies with white guys falling out of them.

Chris Rock

I am actually a big sissy, and growing up, I never used to watch horror movies. 'Bambi' gave me nightmares.

Danielle Panabaker

By going to the movies, and because of other things, too, going to college, making a wide variety of friends, moving around traveling, I became a lot more open-minded than the heritage I was born into might have suggested.

Roger Ebert

The action movies changed radically when it became possible to Velcro your muscles on. It was the beginning of a new era. The visual took over. The special effects became more important than the single person. That was the beginning of the end.

Sylvester Stallone

I remember being on film sets when I was younger, and only men got to do the cool action movies. So I thought, 'Maybe I'll get to produce one day and get to do cool stuff too,' which is what happened when we did 'Charlie's Angels.' Starting my production company was a big turning point for me.

Drew Barrymore

I'd love to win trophies, be in movies, have a body of work I'm proud of and find a way to enjoy it along the way. Success is probably a more of a complicated thing than that.

Demetri Martin

It's like those high-school yearbook photos that everyone would rather not see: Oh my God, look at that mullet hair. I have those photos too, but for me, they're, like, entire movies. And they show them on cable.

John Cusack

I want to turn my attention to movies about love relationships. Exploring the female psyche - there ought to be some interesting discoveries there. Love stories. If you do it right, people want to hear romantic dialog.

Sylvester Stallone

If you look at Indian movies, every time they wanted an exotic locale, they would have a dance number in Kashmir. Kashmir was India's fairyland. Indians went there because in a hot country you go to a cold place. People would be entranced by the sight of snow.

Salman Rushdie

I respect the fact that people have worked hard all week and want to go to the movies on the weekend and be entertained.

Michael Moore

In life and in movies, it's a similar challenge, where you have expectations, and you end up in situations that are not meeting your expectations.

Jeff Bridges

I'm obsessed with zombies. I like watching zombie movies and I read zombie books.

Kevin Bacon

I made some truly awful movies. 'Stop! Or My Mom Will Shoot' was the worst. If you ever want someone to confess to murder just make him or her sit through that film. They will confess to anything after 15 minutes.

Sylvester Stallone

There might have been a period around 'Tango & Cash' when I was nearly fashionable. My problem is that my weight's always been changing for the movies I'm in.

Sylvester Stallone

I love doing normal things - movies, shopping, going out with friends, writing, reading, taking hot bubble baths - that's a big one for relaxation. I also love to go to art and history museums.

Christina Aguilera

My motto: 'No good movie is depressing. All bad movies are depressing.'

Roger Ebert

I think once you enter the dating world and you realise it's nothing like those Disney movies you watched when you were a little girl, you just become more guarded.

Megan Fox

You can't intellectually purge yourself of who you are. Whatever that is, it's going to come out in the wash, the film wash. What you are is going to be relevant, if not to yourself, to the movies you make.

Steven Spielberg

Stephen Hawking's been watching too many Hollywood movies. I think the only kind aliens in Hollywood are the ones created by Steven Spielberg - 'Close Encounters of the Third Kind' and 'E.T.,' for example. All other aliens are trying to suck our brains out.

Neil deGrasse Tyson

One of the nice things about licensing music to movies or advertisements is you can reach a lot of people who normally wouldn't hear music.

Moby

Movies that encourage empathy are more effective than those that objectify problems.

Roger Ebert

I love scary movies. I like blood and gore, and I love Halloween movies.

Carrie Underwood

Sex is a doorway to something so powerful and mystical, but movies usually depict it in a completely flat way.

David Lynch

Horror movies don't exist unless you go and see them, and people always will.

Joss Whedon

I go to the movies a lot, and I regret when I see some actor that I used to like, to find them offering no more surprises.

Catherine Deneuve

I like smart movies about smart people, and enjoy it when most of the facts are on the table and we can contemplate them together.

Roger Ebert

I was born in Paris in the mid-1960s, and by the time I was 12 I had started going to the movies by myself. Most of the movies of that period never appealed to me. I didn't like the 'naturalism,' the sad or the 'down-to-earth' characters. What I wanted from film was fantasy, dreams, funny situations, extravagant decor - and beautiful women.

Christian Louboutin

Not only do I have to live, right, I have to get some cash for my troubles - it's a scary thing, and people need to start to think about the messages that they send in the movies.

Morgan Freeman

People need to start to think about the messages that they send in the movies.

Morgan Freeman

I grew up watching all these crazy movies, European movies and stuff, and I guess that I always laughed at things that were a little more offbeat.

Louis C. K.

If I saw 'Virgin Suicides' or 'Eternal Sunshine,' I'm so proud to be in those movies. They are such great movies. I felt so free on those sets.

Kirsten Dunst

My children have never watched any of my films. Charlie knows that daddy makes movies, but he says they are not good enough for him to watch.

Russell Crowe

I have loved movies as the number one thing in my life so long that I can't ever remember a time when I didn't.

Quentin Tarantino

I'm not a Hollywood basher because enough good movies come out of the Hollywood system every year to justify its existence, without any apologies.

Quentin Tarantino

I'm not a strikingly handsome guy, but I'm in movies.

Shia LaBeouf

The thing with movies is, because you have so little time, I always feel like there are more things we could've done with the character. If we'd done a sequel to 'The Thomas Crown Affair,' what would that have been like? But for the most part, you try not to think of that, because it's just going to break your heart.

Denis Leary

I loved cowboy movies when I was a kid. When I was five years old, I was already wearing a cowboy hat and suit. When I grew up, I knew John Wayne, Clint Eastwood, Kirk Douglas and so on.

Jackie Chan

It's nice that there are movies and songs about romance - it's what motivates us as human beings. I'm all for being brainwashed by rom-coms.

Zooey Deschanel

There's more to life than movies.

Paul Walker

Everyone related to me in my circle was from church: church friends, church school, church activities. All my friends weren't allowed to watch MTV or go to PG-13 movies or listen to the radio, so I didn't really know anything different. That's how I was raised.

Katy Perry

I want to make all kinds of movies. I do want to make big movies that are a lot of fun to go to, but I also want to make movies that are going to stimulate some thought and maybe raise some awareness.

Nicolas Cage

I never really got nightmares from movies. In fact, I recall my father saying when I was three years old that I would be scared, but I never was.

Tim Burton

Even when I was a little kid, I always said I would be in the movies one day, and damned if I didn't make it.

Richard Pryor

To be an artist, you don't have to compose music or paint or be in the movies or write books. It's just a way of living. It has to do with paying attention, remembering, filtering what you see and answering back, participating in life.

Viggo Mortensen

When I got depressed, I watched Bruce Lee movies. I learned everything from Bruce Lee.

Jackie Chan

You do get very tired sometimes, when you're sitting around for hours in movies. You get depleted.

Al Pacino

My mother had to send me to the movies with my birth certificate, so that I wouldn't have to pay the extra fifty cents that the adults had to pay.

Kareem Abdul-Jabbar

The same sensations that you get in heavy metal are in horror movies. Heavy metal sounds evil and horror movies are evil, ha ha!

Kirk Hammett

A lot of people just go to movies that feed into their preexisting and not so noble needs and desires: They just go to action pictures, and things like that.

Roger Ebert

I've never made any horrible, horrible movies. If you don't ruin your reputation, you can always get work.

Bill Murray

I am a giant proponent of giant screens. But I accept the fact that most of my movies are going to be seen on phones.

George Lucas

I'm not a film buff. I don't watch a lot of movies.

Denzel Washington

Bruce Lee was very famous. I watched his movies and he is amazing. He is a martial arts master, his philosophy, his movement, both physically and mentally, were very strong.

Jet Li

I don't like business talkers, you know, people who are constantly like, 'Blah blah blah movies.' I find it incredibly boring.

Zooey Deschanel

I'm not an admirer of action movies. I just think, Oh my God, it must be so tiring.

Catherine Deneuve

During the off-season, I go to the movies almost every day.

Derek Jeter

I go to movies expecting to have a whole experience. If I want a movie that doesn't end, I'll go to a French movie. That's a betrayal of trust to me. A movie has to be complete within itself; it can't just build off the first one or play variations.

Joss Whedon

I think that's what distinguishes Schmidt, really. In the movies now, so much of what is appealing to an audience is the dramatic or has to do with science fiction, and Schmidt is simply human. There's no melodrama; there's no device, It's just about a human being.

Jack Nicholson

I like all of the mental, psychological thriller movies too. I enjoy horror movies across the board.

Sophia Bush

Movies are not about the weekend that they're released, and in the grand scheme of things, that's probably the most unimportant time of a film's life.

Quentin Tarantino

It's simple: You get a part. You play a part. You play it well. You do your work and you go home. And what is wonderful about movies is that once they're done, they belong to the people. Once you make it, it's what they see. That's where my head is at.

Denzel Washington

My grandmother and I saw an average of eight movies a week, double features, second run.

Carol Burnett

Most of the time it's the role. Sometimes it's the story and sometimes it just the paycheck. It's the little movies that come out as stories or the fact that I have work to go out, you know what I'm saying, you can only be out so long without work, you start getting antsy.

Morgan Freeman

Being alone is scarier than any boogey man and the reason why I don't choose to see Horror movies as a rule.

Tom Sizemore

All my movies are achingly personal.

Quentin Tarantino

My mom took me to see Carnal Knowledge and The Wild Bunch and all these kind of movies when I was a kid.

Quentin Tarantino

When my mother got home from work, she would take me to the movies. It was her way of getting out, and she would take me with her. I'd go home and act all the parts. It had a tremendous influence on my becoming an actor.

Al Pacino

I have a very busy life, and not many people who have a career and four kids go out a lot to the movies.

Meryl Streep

I don't have too many plans filled out. I know I want to keep doing more music. I've got a couple of albums worth of songs I'd like to put it out there. As far as movies, I just want to continue how I've been doing it: working with terrific people is certainly on my agenda, and then doing stories that interest me.

Jeff Bridges

I think all of us, under certain circumstances, could be capable of some very despicable acts. And that's why, over the years, in my movies I've had characters who didn't care what people thought about them. We try to be as true to them as possible and maybe see part of ourselves in there that we may not like.

Martin Scorsese

My wife comes with me on all the movies, but she is not an appendage to a film star or anything like that. She is a completely intertwined partner. She is the other half of me. Also, we're still very much in love with each other. We always have been, we always will be.

Michael Caine

A lot of the struggle I had with movies is I really loved moments and tones and feelings in a scene, and I loved creating those, but I never really had great stories to string them together.

Louis C. K.

Sundance is weird. The movies are weird - you actually have to think about them when you watch them.

Britney Spears

The person that made me want to make movies, and the reason I do films, is Bruce Lee. He was an incredible actor, and he had a lot of charisma. Handsome, action, you know, everything was there. I loved Bruce Lee.

LL Cool J

An often-repeated assertion in the body of film criticism I have written is the assertion that movies do not just mirror the culture of any given time; they also create it.

bell hooks

One of my gripes about movies is that people take them so seriously, and the moneymaking aspects are so brutal.

Bill Murray

We all need illusions. That's why we love movies.

Monica Bellucci

I loved old black and white movies, especially the Fred Astaire and Ginger Rogers musicals. I loved everything about them - the songs, the music, the romance and the spectacle. They were real class and I knew that I wanted to be in that world.

Sharon Stone

I look at the Christian Bale movies, the 'Batman' films, and that shows you that superhero movies don't just have to be about men in tights.

James McAvoy

We don't make glamorous movies today. Everything now is very realistic, artistic - and depressing. When is the last time you you saw a wonderful musical or a fabulous fantasy?

Edith Head

When I was growing up, I was the most pretentious person I have ever met. I only read obscure books and watched obscure movies and only listened to obscure music.

Moby

Basically, one of the hardest things about being an actor is getting your first break. I'm a product of nepotism. The doors were open to me. I'd done several movies before I decided what I wanted to do.

Jeff Bridges

I'm certainly curious about people. As a kid, I moved around a lot. I was raised in a lot of different places, and thanks to working in the movies, I've gotten to keep traveling. I've always been interested in other cultures and languages.

Viggo Mortensen

How do people relate to movies now, when they're on portable devices or streaming them? It's not as much about going to the movies. That experience has changed.

Keanu Reeves

Everybody wants blockbusters. I like to see a few pictures now and then that have to do with people and have relationships, and that's what I want to do films about. I don't want to see these sci-fi movies, and I don't want to do one of those. I don't understand it.

James Garner

I like the George Romero films, which were really great, social satire movies; really twisted.

John Cusack

It's important to me that I don't get trapped in the whole teen scene, because I feel that you can get lost in those kind of movies, and they aren't really about the actors; they're about the selling of the concept, and how much money it makes.

Kirsten Dunst

I love indie movies. I think that independent cinema is where it's at and where a lot of trends begin. It's where new filmmakers are breaking through.

Zooey Deschanel

On television and in the movies, crimes are always solved. Nothing is left uncertain. By the end, the viewer knows whodunit. In real life, on the other hand, many murders remain unsolved, and even some that are 'solved' to the satisfaction of the police and prosecutors lack sufficient evidence to result in a conviction.

Alan Dershowitz

I said, 'I'm going to the United States to study with Stella Adler and do movies because nobody here has done it and my passion is films.' But I came here and I didn't speak English, I didn't have a green card, I didn't know I had to have an agent, I couldn't drive, I was dyslexic.

Salma Hayek

There's no difference between movies and television. None at all. Except in a lot of cases, television's much better than movies.

George Lucas

The reason I chose the movies that I did was based on where they were being filmed.

Meryl Streep

I missed out on everything. Sometimes on the street I see teenagers hanging out and going to the movies, going to concerts, and I get so jealous.

Adriana Lima

Kids end up seeing my movies anyway but some of the mothers get mad at me so I figured I'd make one that I can't get yelled at for.

Adam Sandler

Movies are hard work. The public doesn't see that. The critics don't see it. But they're a lot of work. A lot of work.

Robert De Niro

I want a lot of people to see my movies. More black people. More white people. I want to make that connection.

Tyler Perry

Why be boring? Have some fun. Rock shows should be like movies: I don't go to a movie hoping it'll change my life.

Alice Cooper

Hollywood is throwing action movies at me.

Liam Neeson

Making movies, you're like an independent contractor - you come in, you have a specific job, and a lot of what you do is completely manipulated, which is good and bad.

Zooey Deschanel

How many movies do you see when you can say this director really knew what film he wanted to make? I can count them on the fingers of one hand.

Gary Oldman

I don't want to make movies for kids, and I don't want to make movies for adults either.

Kristen Stewart

I didn't know what types of movies I wanted to do. I want to do things that are different. I want to take my time with each role.

Leonardo DiCaprio

I just want to keep doing what I'm doing and hopefully people will watch my movies.

Leonardo DiCaprio

Basically, there's not enough sex in movies, that's it. I'm trying to say it, people. I miss sex in movies because sex is natural, guns are not.

Zoe Saldana

Where I live, nobody who's fourteen is having sex and doing major drugs. And I think if you see it in the movies, you may be influenced by it. I think it's so important to preserve your innocence.

Natalie Portman

I was studying to be an architect, I wasn't plotting to join the movies. Films were just another career option. I took acting up with the same schoolgirl enthusiasm I had for examinations. Acting is a job and I take it very seriously.

Aishwarya Rai Bachchan

I love family films. Of course, as a mother who has to watch so many movies, you really appreciate it when somebody makes a film that is for everybody - family entertainment that's really for the family, where everyone has a good time.

Salma Hayek

I don't know why I don't watch a lot of movies; I can barely keep up with the things my friends are in. There isn't enough time in life.

Meryl Streep

I don't blame folks for not wanting to put me in their movies or whatever. I understand if their audiences had an association with me.

Joseph Gordon-Levitt

One of the reasons why people - particularly young people - love action movies is because what they are really looking for is justice.

Steven Seagal

If I did any movies I'd have to take a break from singing, because I'd want it to be really good.

Justin Timberlake

I wouldn't like to be in movies. Movie people are strange. They live a different life than musicians do.

Stevie Nicks

James Cagney, Steve McQueen, I loved all those guys. I grew up loving the movies but had no desire to be in them.

Mark Wahlberg

If you make action movies, the critics will savage you, and then your movies are outdated the following week with the new wave of special effects.

Adam McKay

I just knew that was what I wanted to do. I was going to perform as a singer; I was going to perform as a dancer, and I was, you know, going to do movies and be an actress. I was going to do it or die trying. That's what my life was.

Jennifer Lopez

Without a doubt, I was born to want to make cinema, but the kind of cinema I want to make is not like commercial movies, which I enjoy myself, but I wanted to be the kind of filmmaker who wrote original work, sort of like a novelist would who deals with who we are and our times or our relationships.

Francis Ford Coppola

I was never into the popular school or clique or anything. Then I started doing movies when I was in high school, so then I got popular. Then the girls paid attention to you who didn't before.

John Cusack

I just think old old movies, they make you concentrate and pay attention so much more. They feel so warm. A lot of modern digital videotape, it's just too bright. Don't know why, it's not warm.

Jack White

You make movies for the people. If critics happen to like

them too, well, that's a home run.

Vin Diesel

When I was a little girl, I watched all old movies. My
mother liked old movies, and she loved shopping for
antiques, so I was around old things all the time.

Dita Von Teese

I don't know many women who can relate to Sharon Stone
and the kind of movies she does. I don't know a lot of guys
who can relate to Tom Cruise's movies because they're on
a kind of fantastic level. I like movies I can relate to.

Kim Cattrall

American actors who voice animated movies are so
brilliant at it, because by the nature of American speak, it's
full of energy and full of commitment. And as a British
actor, we have to kind of learn that.

Helen Mirren

Most filmmakers' entire body of knowledge is of other
movies. When they describe things, they describe them in
relation to other movies. That's why we have so many
cyclical movies that look like other movies. But I'm not

cynical. I even go to some of those movies.

John Malkovich

It's hard to get movie studios to pay a lot of money for movies that don't have robots or explosions.

John Green

Sometimes when we weep in the movies we weep for ourselves or for a life unlived. Or we even go to the movies because we want to resist the emotion that's there in front of us. I think there is always a catharsis that I look for and that makes the movie experience worthwhile.

Edward Zwick

You know when you watch old movies, it's always the small parts you remember, the character actors who come in like a breath of fresh air.

Amy Sedaris

I don't make movies because I love to act. I make movies because I like to make movies, and I like to be a part of that process.

Jodie Foster

Movies are open doors, and at every door, I change character and life.

Juliette Binoche

I crave working on those small independent movies because I love going to see those myself.

Orlando Bloom

Acting is a bit like being an athlete. You spend all your time getting ready to do something for two minutes. All the things that made my career in the movies happen took two or three minutes, which is the time that it takes for a 'take'. In that time, something happens. That's what people know you for, just like someone running the hundred metres.

Christopher Walken

I used to be prettier than I am, but I think I look better now. I was a pretty boy. Particularly in my early movies. I don't like looking at them so much. There's a sort of pretty thing about me.

Christopher Walken

I've made movies that I thought were okay, but then I was very good. And sometimes you're in a movie and you think, 'I wish more people saw that' - because you're good. And it just works out that the movie gets lost. But that's show business.

Christopher Walken

I moved to California when I was twelve and I got a video camera and made little movies because I didn't have any friends yet. I would force my sister to make these movies with me - which became my YouTube channel.

Dylan O'Brien

Well, I think one of the main things that you have to think about when acting in the movies is to try not to make the acting show.

James Stewart

Well, Toronto, I consider to be the birthplace of my films. I've made three films and this is the third one to premiere here in the same theater on the same day at the same time - they are my audience. They're the people that I think about while I'm writing, directing, and editing. I specifically make movies for them.

Jason Reitman

You can't work in the movies. Movies are all about lighting. Very few filmmakers will concentrate on the story. You get very little rehearsal time, so anything you do onscreen is a kind of speed painting.

John Malkovich

Some people think literature is high culture and that it should only have a small readership. I don't think so... I have to compete with popular culture, including TV, magazines, movies and video games.

Haruki Murakami

I was never interested in being powerful or famous. But once I got to film school and learned about movies, I just fell in love with it. I didn't care what kind of movies I made.

George Lucas

People don't have these tidy little redemption arcs in reality the way they do in movies.

Diablo Cody

I definitely want to act, but I also want to score movies, and I have this idea to fuse classical music with other styles that would give it a different perception.

Alicia Keys

We make the kind of movies we like to watch. I love to laugh. I love to be amazed by how beautiful it is. But I also love to be moved to tears. There's lots of heart in our films.

John Lasseter

The best movies have one sentence that they're exploring, a thesis, something that people can argue about over dinner afterward.

Helen Hunt

People feel the worst film I made was 'Jack.' But to this day, when I get checks from old movies I've made, 'Jack' is one of the biggest ones. No one knows that. If people hate the movie, they hate the movie. I just wanted to work with Robin Williams.

Francis Ford Coppola

If I make two movies my entire life, and they're two movies that - whether they make a lot of money or two people go to see them - they speak of me, then I consider them incredibly successful. I don't need to be Steven Spielberg.

Jodie Foster

Even today, in our progressive times, in most movies that come out, the men have to have biceps and the women have to be thin or something.

Joseph Gordon-Levitt

Comedy. It was just huge in my house. Peter Sellers and Alec Guinness, Monty Python and all those James Bond movies were highly regarded.

Mike Myers

I'm not too proud of the movies I made as a grownup except for 'That Hagen Girl', which nobody remembers but which gave me a chance to act.

Shirley Temple

And if people come up and say they like the movies you're in, it's a great compliment.

Jason Statham

The 'serial kisser' tag that has been thrust on to me is a lame stereotype. It irritates me. Yes, there is sexual content in my movies, and I have never been apologetic about doing bold scenes. But it's not fair to tag me this way because that can be very stifling.

Emraan Hashmi

I spent a lot of my twenties wanting a maid, really. I thought I wanted a relationship, but I just wanted somebody to fix and nurse me, and I'd take her hostage for six months. When you're 23, 24, you want to be in a relationship because they look brilliant - you've heard all the songs about it and seen all the movies and it looks great.

Robbie Williams

Saturday night at my house, I often trot out classic movies and force the urchins to watch them. There is much wailing and gnashing of teeth, but I think it's important to teach kids about American culture, and films are certainly a big part of it.

Bill O'Reilly

Books and movies are different art forms with different

rules. And because of that, they never translate exactly.

Tom Clancy

I had to act in a school play when I was about ten years old. I really didn't want to do it. But everyone had to do it so I didn't have a choice. A talent agent came and watched it and later gave me some work. It's funny because I'd always known that I wanted a movie career. I just didn't think that I would be in the movies.

Kristen Stewart

I don't know what it was, maybe the movie theaters in my immediate surrounding neighbourhood in Burbank, but I never saw what would be considered A movies.

Tim Burton

I grew up in Toronto and as long as I can remember, as long as there was cable, even those old cable boxes that were wired to the TV, there have been Bollywood movies on Toronto TV.

Mike Myers

It may be true that the only reason the comic book industry now exists is for this purpose, to create characters for movies, board games and other types of merchandise.

Alan Moore

I'm in a play on Broadway, I have an animated TV show coming up, I have a few movies that just came out.

Neil Patrick Harris

And I love Mel Brooks. My Dad loved his movies, too, they're awesome, the kind of thing that if you're in for ten minutes, you're in for two hours.

Mike Myers

People talk about mumblecore but I prefer bumblecore, hyper-realistic bee movies about how bees really are.

Mindy Kaling

I've never held myself up particularly high when I had movies that worked, and I never held myself all that low when I had failures.

Ben Affleck

My dad had a commercial film company, so he had a

videotape player before anyone. So he got Mel Brooks movies or Citizen Kane or some classic old movies. And every summer the revival house in Evanston would show the great films from the '50s and '60s and '70s.

John Cusack

Twenty years ago my parents wouldn't know who the X-Men were, and now everybody knows that stuff. It means that deconstruction of the superhero is something you can do. All those movies have led to a point where we can finally have 'Watchmen' with a Superman character who doesn't want to save the world and a Batman who has trouble in bed.

Zack Snyder

I don't like cursing in movies. I feel like cursing has become the new hackiness. You try to find substitutions for cursing.

Zach Galifianakis

Some disaster movies look like you're watching someone else play video games. They're fun but it's not real.

Eli Roth

They allow us to disrespect our Black woman. A lot of these things would be considered criminal if it were to be carried out in the streets. That's like when they tell you after you buy your VHS and you rent movies they tell you not to copy the movies.

Afrika Bambaataa

I loved all movies, literally. I certainly loved 'Shane' and 'Roxie Hart.' Later on, when I was less of a kid, I loved 'L'Avventura' and 'Persona' and all Fellini movies and like everybody else I loved John Ford. Then and now, I loved Preston Sturges, maybe above anyone.

Mike Nichols

I don't get it when you get so much openness about the way movies are made, and the special effects and the behind-the-scenes stuff and all of that. I can't help but feel like this reduces it a little bit.

Christian Bale

I think there's a vague sense out there that movies are becoming more and more unreal. I know I've felt it.

Christopher Nolan

It's a funny thing: You want so badly for people to see what you do - you're proud of it - and I like the effect that movies have on people. But the attention can also make me uncomfortable.

Kristen Stewart

Movies such as 'Citizen Kane' and 'The Front Page' portrayed an era when driven newspapermen would do anything to get a story. The U.K.'s rough-and-tumble Fleet Street remains something of a throwback to that era, as demonstrated by the recent phone-hacking scandal - which led to the demise of yet another century-old paper, the 'News of the World.'

Nathan Myhrvold

We're more familiar with what economists call an English auction - prices start low and rise as people bid. However, there is also the Dutch auction, where prices start high and go lower until somebody bites. Movies are sold to the audience via a very slow Dutch auction, where each phase between price drops can last weeks or months.

Nathan Myhrvold

I feel like it's harder to get women to show up for movies.

Tina Fey

I had a certain career as an actor that I think was quite personal as well, and had a lot of integrity, but I wasn't writing my own things or directing my own movies.

Jodie Foster

Now, there are so many movies, so many festivals, and so many awards going on, each judged with each other, like your work is worse than others and that's not fair. How can you tell what's best and what's worst from these awards? We're talking about art.

Javier Bardem

'Tropic Thunder' is one of my favorite movies of all time. 'Blazing Saddles.' Anything that will get me to smile.

John Cena

The irony is that you can't use real rain to make movies.

Greg Kinnear

You know when Hollywood does a great big blockbuster that really wraps you up in a world, and lets you believe in extraordinary things that move you in some way, in an almost operatic sensibility? That to me is the most fun I have at the movies.

Christopher Nolan

Before I was an actor, I was never able to hold a job for more than 3 months for some reason. It just wouldn't hold my interest, so there was some way that I wound up quitting or getting fired from it. But being an actor is perfect, because movies usually take about three months to shoot. Then it's over and they say, 'Hey, great job!'

Dennis Quaid

I have a great job writing for 'The Office,' but, really, all television writers do is dream of one day writing movies. I'll put it this way: At the Oscars the most famous person in the room is, like, Angelina Jolie. At the Emmys the huge exciting celebrity is Bethenny Frankel. You get what I mean.

Mindy Kaling

People called '28 Days' and '28 Weeks' zombie movies, and they're not! It's some sort of virus; they're not dead.

George A. Romero

When we were doing 'Freaks and Geeks', I didn't quite understand how movies and TV worked, and I would improvise even if the camera wasn't on me. I thought I was helping the other actors by keeping them on their toes, but nobody appreciated it when I would trip them up. So I was improvising a little bit back then, but not in a productive way.

James Franco

'Black Swan' does what Hollywood movies have always done - it spends its energies on getting some surface things right while getting everything important wrong. Darren Aronofsky, the director, applies the same techniques and the same sensibility here as he did with 'The Wrestler,' only with a prettier protagonist.

Robert Gottlieb

I'm actually scared of horror movies. I'm kind of Scaredy Cat when it comes to that stuff.

Jennifer Love Hewitt

The only thing I can't do is hear. I can drive, I have a life with four kids, I work on TV, I do movies, so the deafness question, is it that they want to know because, what? Not sure.

Marlee Matlin

I feel like a lot of the female relationships I see on TV or in movies are in some way free of the kind of jealousy and anxiety and posturing that has been such a huge part of my female friendships, which I hope lessens a little bit with age.

Lena Dunham

When I started to watch some of the films I'd done, I realized I was doing movies that I might not actually want to see.

Heath Ledger

But most good movies have a gun in them.

David Sedaris

The one regret I have about my own abortions is that they cost money that might otherwise have been spent on something more pleasurable, like taking the kids to movies and theme parks.

Barbara Ehrenreich

There's an absolute prejudice that good movies are dramas and comedies are more dismissable. But I couldn't disagree more.

Joseph Gordon-Levitt

I like Ryan Gosling as an actor. I watch all of his movies, and he's Canadian and I just like his swag. I read his interviews and I'm a big fan of his.

Drake

If dreams are like movies, then memories are films about ghosts.

Adam Duritz

The more technology we introduce into society, the more people will aggregate, will want to be with other people: movies, rock concerts, shopping.

John Naisbitt

Going to the movies was a big event in my youth. My father would be the initiator - he'd have me put on a jacket to see a film.

Ralph Fiennes

I want to make movies that pierce people's hearts and touch them in some way, even if it's just for the night while they're in the cinema; in that moment, I want to bring actual tears to their eyes and goosebumps to their skin.

Russell Crowe

I did 'Are We There Yet?' because I wanted to do a movie for my fans' kids. Black kids don't really see movies on this budget for them, starring them. And there's so many white kids that love that movie.

Ice Cube

I've done movies for certain reasons; I did 'Anaconda' because the black man lives. Simple. The black man isn't dead in the first three pages, like Jurassic Park. It's like, 'The black man kills the snake with a Latino girl? Damn! I got to do this.'

Ice Cube

Movies, as evidenced by a chorus of protesting and celebrating Americans, influence broader trends.

Anna Deavere Smith

My favorite thing about movies is the ending, and so all my favorite movies have really great endings.

Emma Stone

My family and our neighbors and friends thought of Africa and its Africans as extensions of the stereotyped characters that we saw in movies and on television in films such as 'Tarzan' and in programs such as 'Ramar of the Jungle' and 'Sheena, Queen of the Jungle.'

Henry Louis Gates

Average Americans order nonfat decaf iced vanilla lattes at Starbucks and choose from 1,500 drawer pulls at The Great Indoors. Amazon gives every town a bookstore with 2 million titles, while Netflix promises 35,000 different movies on DVD. Choice is everywhere - liberating to some, but to others, a new source of stress.

Virginia Postrel

Most of us cluster somewhere in the middle of most statistical distributions. But there are lots of bell curves, and pretty much everyone is on a tail of at least one of them. We may collect strange memorabilia or read esoteric books, hold unusual religious beliefs or wear odd-sized shoes, suffer rare diseases or enjoy obscure movies.

Virginia Postrel

The profusion of fonts is one more product of the digital revolution. Beginning in the mid-'80s and accelerating in the 1990s, type design weathered the sort of radical, technology-driven transformation that other creative industries, including music, publishing, and movies, now face.

Virginia Postrel

Denzel Washington has a great sense of humor. He did all those 'Nutty Professor' movies.

Seth MacFarlane

I don't make the best movies in the world, but at times, I do feel like I'm adding something to the cinematic community.

Seth Rogen

I'm terrible at horror movies, by the way. I get scared so easily.

Oliver Stone

Who doesn't know about Bollywood? After all, we churn out movies in such great quantities every year! People across the globe know Shekhar Kapur.

Arjun Rampal

I was sick and tired of being an English actor who did a lot of American movies because I was cheap and good.

Daniel Craig

I go to the movies at least five times a week, and after a while everything becomes a blur to me.

David Sedaris

Growing up, I always loved Disney movies, but the first movie I remember seeing is 'Sleepers,' so I wasn't really taken to children's movies.

Sarah Silverman

I like the idea of working in different genres and transcending genres and hopefully finding success, and ultimately make movies people like.

Dwayne Johnson

Now, if you are like me - if you are like practically anybody in America - then you probably hold some negative opinions about the French, based upon movies, rumors, recent headlines, unfortunate run-ins with Parisian waiters, or... you know... all that unpleasantness surrounding the Vichy regime.

Elizabeth Gilbert

If your movies don't perform, they just stop calling you.

Matt Damon

I love music, and after my first experience with movies, I can't wait to do more.

Rihanna

Listen, I think movies serve many different purposes, from those movies that are frivolous and just an entertainment, to movies that just go to exploring the complexities of the human soul. Everything is valid if it's done with honesty and dignity, and I actually do both of those types of movies in my career.

Antonio Banderas

I hope that I would be considered romantic. I don't know...

one of my favorite movies is 'The Notebook' so I guess that would be considered romantic. But I think being romantic is more than the flowers and the gifts. It's about connecting with the person and being able to talk and share things with her.

Taylor Lautner

I like to think the movies that I've picked have something worthwhile to say. Something relevant.

Mark Ruffalo

Everything we have today that's cool comes from someone wanting more of something they loved in the past. Action figures, videogames, superhero movies, iPods: All are continuations of a love that wanted more.

Patton Oswalt

I was never that into the movies. Never. Even as a youngster. I became interested in movie music only because of the studio orchestras in Hollywood.

John Williams

We ogle plants and animals up close on television, the Internet and in the movies. We may not worship the animals we see, but we still regard them as necessary physical and spiritual companions. Technological nature can't completely satisfy that yearning.

Diane Ackerman

What bugs me is that movies don't reflect how interesting and vibrant women are. We don't treasure women as they get older.

Jill Clayburgh

I love 'Paranormal Activity' and 'The Exorcist.' 'The Shining' is a great one too, but there's not a lot that scares me. Maybe it's because I know the other side of it, and I know how movies are made, but it takes a lot for me to get freaked out.

Lucy Hale

The tension I feel is the moment they say, 'Action!' Movies are like lightning in a bottle, and you always want to find when you possibly can catch a surprising moment.

Annette Bening

I'm the most inappropriate dad. I curse in front of my kids and their friends. I let my kids watch R-rated movies. I'll walk by the movie theater and say, 'Let's go see that,' and my kids will say, 'No, it's rated R. It's not appropriate for kids.' I'm like Uncle Dad. We have fun. I don't live with them, but I drive over four days a week.

Marlon Wayans

I like the good feeling movies.

Robert Duvall

'St. Elmo's Fire' is one of my favorite films. I like the storytelling of those teenage American films. You don't get that now. Teenage American movies are all about sick jokes, puking a lot, arse jokes.

James McAvoy

I look at myself as an audience member. I still love movies, and I still go and sit in the back of the big dark room with everybody else, and I want the same thrill.

Samuel L. Jackson

Horror movies started to wane around the onset of World War II, and after World War II, when all the troops came home, people weren't really interested in seeing horror movies, because they had the real horror right on their front doorsteps.

Kirk Hammett

I've been in enough movies to know that when you're on the set and you start shooting, you're looking at playback and you get a sense of what it's going to be like.

Mark Wahlberg

In my movies, I'm not trying to erase any old image of myself, really. And also I'm not trying to imitate anyone or follow in their footsteps, because I know, Burt Reynolds was just one of the people that told me this, I know how you can only last in this business if you got something special to offer, just by being yourself.

Mark Wahlberg

A huge part of acting in movies is appetite. You do your best work when you've got a lot of appetite and you really want to embrace something. When you get tired, you don't have that hunger.

Clive Owen

The best movies now are called 'thrillers.' Because if you use the word 'horror,' people's associations are straight-to-video crap.

Eli Roth

I keep telling people I'll make movies until I'm fifty and then I'll go and do something else. I'm going to be a professional gentleman of leisure.

Eddie Murphy

We did six records, then six movies. Now we need to do six of something else, so we get 666 - and then our master Satan can return!

Cheech Marin

He's my favorite! He wrote and produced, and starred in and cast all of his movies! Can you imagine? I get really excited when I talk about Charlie Chaplin.

Emma Stone

The stereotype of psychotherapy portrayed in popular books and movies is lying on the couch and saying whatever comes into your mind, while a kindly psychoanalyst listens and nods knowingly from time to time. After years and years, something wonderful is supposed to happen.

David D. Burns

Nostalgia, the vice of the aged. We watch so many old movies our memories come in monochrome.

Angela Carter

I have a to-do list and I have a farm I care for, and things I like to do for fun - going to movies and all that stuff. It's a painfully normal life!

Brad Paisley

I think with the success of, like, every summer there has been a couple R-rated comedies that have done so well; I think it is so nice to see that people are turning out to see these movies, and it doesn't seem to be as big a stigma with the studios anymore.

Will Ferrell

The tour bus is always fun, and there's plenty of time to watch movies. Actually, Kanye introduced me to the movie 'Step Brothers.' We were sitting there, watching it and clowning around - it was so funny, man.

Kid Cudi

I loved all those classic figures from the '30s and '40s...
Bette Davis, Joan Crawford, Humphrey Bogart, Rita
Hayworth. They had such glamour and style. I loved the
movies of those times too - so much attention paid to
details, lights, clothing, the way the studios would develop
talent.

Grace Jones

I haven't deliberately set out to play the blonde bombshell
in my movies. In fact, it's probably been quite the opposite.
After the success of The Mask, I wasn't offered all that
many blonde bombshell parts, to be honest. I think people
believed from the beginning that I could actually walk and
talk at the same time.

Cameron Diaz

In all honesty I think that I've had a very normal life, even
though I've been making movies since I was 9.

Josh Hutcherson

In Chinese culture, it wouldn't occur to kids to question or
talk back to their parents. In American culture, kids in
books, TV shows and movies constantly score points with
their snappy back talk. Typically, it's the parents who need

to be taught a life lesson - by their children.

Amy Chua

I believe that movies are fast becoming antique and dinosauric as a medium. Film is a medium for the over-40s and television has gone the same way. If you're going to look towards the new generation, then of course you're going to have to be a lot more random, spontaneous, irreverent and provocative with your programming.

Malcolm Mclaren

It's true - women want the fantasy. So give them romance - but without the desperation, wondering, and waiting you see in the movies.

Nadine Velazquez

I definitely have found a balance. I've had so many offers in the past to do different movies or different things and I always choose tournaments over it.

Serena Williams

I would do anything for a part, nearly anything. Being in movies doesn't mean being pretty.

Diane Kruger

The reason I keep making movies is I hate the last thing I did. I'm trying to rectify my wrongs.

Joaquin Phoenix

I get inspired when I look at Tom Lennon, who did 'Reno 911!' for six seasons while writing huge movies and directing and also doing other pilots; he did that FX pilot, the 'Star Trek' thing.

Scott Aukerman

I was a total athlete. I loved sports, but when I realized I wasn't going to be a professional athlete, I realized I wanted to be in movies.

Seann William Scott

I tried so hard with movies like Vertigo and Middle of the Night and others. I felt those would show me that it's only a matter of time before I'd find the right one to reach out and touch people.

Kim Novak

Movies are open doors, and at every door, I change character and life... I live for the present always. I accept this risk. I don't deny the past, but it's a page to turn.

Juliette Binoche

My mother was keen that I complete my graduation and never ever wanted me to be in the movies, as my father had made five films that lost money. One of the films he made was 'Agneepath,' which was hugely hyped but underwhelming at the box office, and I remember that my dad had to sell my grandmother's flat to pay off the loan.

Karan Johar

When I was old enough to go to movies alone, I got to see 'Frankenstein' and 'Dracula' on the big screen. I just fell in love with them.

George A. Romero

But in the back of my mind I've always looked to the biggest-scale Hollywood movies. Because to me the most satisfying experience is of watching a movie, if it's done really well. And so that aspiration is always it for me, if I have the opportunity to do it.

Christopher Nolan

I wouldn't trade my career with anybody's. I'd trade a few movies with Tom Hanks - 'Apollo 13' and 'Forrest Gump' - but other than that, I love my career.

John Travolta

It's not that I am not emotional, but I am extremely secure and curb it, as I am afraid to let go and be broken. So, I have cultivated myself to be detached in life, specially where movies are concerned.

Ranbir Kapoor

For me, relationships are the real action movies. Bombs are exploding every day and the kitchen is Ground Zero.

Michelle Williams

I'm like the luckiest girl in the world. I've gotten to be a princess, I've gotten to work with the Muppets. A lot of my childhood dreams about who I wanted to be when I was a grown-up, I at least get to play them in movies.

Amy Adams

I love to unwind and watch movies, especially those from the classic black-and-white era.

Fred Savage

Movies don't make people act a fool. People act a fool because they want to act a fool.

Eazy-E

I think it's more interesting to see people who don't feel appropriately. I relate to that, because sometimes I don't feel anything at all for things I'm supposed to, and other times I feel too much. It's not always like it is in the movies.

Ryan Gosling

My choices in projects have all been character or role-based, and on a financial level, it's obvious: as an actor on a TV series, I get a wonderful paycheck, and a consistent paycheck, which doesn't always happen when you're doing theater or movies.

Jim Parsons

No film has captivated my imagination more than 'King Kong.' I'm making movies today because I saw this film when I was 9 years old.

Peter Jackson

As women, we tend to take the easy way out in showbiz. I have done movies where all I did was look pretty in every frame.

Bipasha Basu

People love teen movies because everyone can relate.

Zoe Kravitz

When I do stand-up for a long time, I'll get burned out, then I'll get an acting gig. For me, the grass is always greener. I'd like to do a mixture of all of it. My goal is just to do small movies that I've written. That's what I'm trying to do now, just write smaller movies.

Zach Galifianakis

People are patronizing the theatres with renewed enthusiasm - there is an entire picnic-like attitude when families go out to see movies, which is a very good sign. They want to see larger-than-life characters on the big screen and not just watch movies on television or on DVDs.

Salman Khan

I grew up watching those blaxploitation movies. Ron O'Neal, Richard Roundtree, Jim Brown, Pam Grier. For the first time, I saw 'The Negro' get one over on 'The Man.'

Samuel L. Jackson

I mean, movies in general tend to sort of portray time, space and identity as these very solid things. Time moves forward. Space is what it is. You are you, and you're always you.

Joseph Gordon-Levitt

Bathroom humor, fart, and poo poo humor in movies gets a laugh. It's a pretty easy audience, and that's been around for ages.

Selma Blair

I don't rehearse a lot. I try to keep it organic. Even in movies, the less I rehearse, the better I am.

Kristen Wiig

I have a trophy case that contains all the action figures ever made of me. It also has items I've stolen from my movies, like three guns and holsters from 'Serenity'.

Nathan Fillion

I like making sci-fi movies because I like watching sci-fi movies. I like watching horror. I like being in a horror movie. I'm a fan. My perspective's a little different just because I get to participate as well as spectate.

Nathan Fillion

If military movies were automatically successful we'd make nothing but military movies. But seriously, patriotism is one thing that all Americans have in common.

Tommy Lee Jones

The Bollywood distribution system is so corrupt that they have trouble making money off movies. So they sell shoes that an actress stepped in. If they turned up the amps some, maybe they could sell the actresses.

Bruce Sterling

In my movies, there has been little to do in the way of animal rights. I have never worked in a movie with animals. No horse-riding, no trained dogs, lions, bears. A few actors, but what could I do? We had to have them.

Casey Affleck

I used to like to set different film clips to classical music, not even my own songs, but make little movies.

Lana Del Rey

Making movies is a very different experience in a lot of ways. It's difficult when you're used to owning the copyright and having a landlord's possessory rights - I rent my plays to the companies that do them and, if I'm upset, I can pull the play. But the only two directors I've worked with are pretty great.

Tony Kushner

I wouldn't call myself successful, just obsessively exhausted. The music makes me smile, the movies make me feel humbled, and the comedy saves my life every day.

Vir Das

I honestly don't love the Cheech and Chong movies, I've got to say.

Seth Rogen

For some people, the highlight of their entire month could

be going out and eating a pizza or watching a movie at a multiplex, and here I am visiting four countries in a month. So, in that way, movies have made me socially aware. I now know how simple people live their lives.

Sonam Kapoor

It's always been my dream to just continually do really cool indie movies, character-driven stuff. I would love to do more theater on a larger scale. I'm just excited for the next thing that comes along that I'm salivating over. I think a little more guerrilla would be really exciting to me.

Tatiana Maslany

It's the contemporary woman that movies don't know what to do with, other than bathe her in a bridal glow in romantic comedies where both the romance and the comedy are artificial sweeteners.

James Wolcott

When I was a little kid - and even still - I loved magic tricks. When I saw how movies got made - at least had a glimpse when I went on the Universal Studios tour with my grandfather, I remember feeling like this was another means by which I could do magic.

J. J. Abrams

I believe in my privacy. I always have, and I always will. I don't think that my private life needs to be on display for me to get a better response at the box office or for me to get a better choice of movies.

Kajol

I can't stand on a podium and beat my chest saying I'm the best. I just think I've been the luckiest of all. Yes, I'm talented. The movies that I've chosen and the way they've fared have also helped. I've always done films I would love to watch. I have stayed away from films which I thought were depressing.

Kajol

We live in an age when it is cheaper to buy the rights to movies than to make them.

Hayao Miyazaki

In terms of television and movies, I've been really interested in seeing the partnership of comedy and beauty and heart. I think they can go together really well and really thoughtfully. But, I'm a total one-hour drama addict. I think when you're a comedian, you tend towards dramas because that's the less stressful thing to watch.

Sarah Silverman

In the movies, I loved Errol Flynn whether he was playing a soldier or a pirate. I dug pirates. In fact, my first exposure to live performances was when my paternal grandfather took me to a D'Oyly Carte performance of 'The Pirates of Penzance' which impresario Sol Hurok imported from London. I loved every minute of it.

Stephen Lang

Movies these days have made killers into funny people. What's that all about? I've got kids and family and friends, and I don't like bad things. I don't think they're funny, and it's irresponsible to make movies that don't show you how that's not good.

Billy Bob Thornton

I'm aware of 'Twilight,' but I've never seen the movies or read any of the books. Frankly, the story leaves me cold - why do a vampire story about abstinence?

Alan Ball

People go to movies on Saturday to get away from the war in Iraq and taxes and election news and pedophiles online and just go and have some fun. I like doing movies that are fun.

Samuel L. Jackson

A lot of the main characters in horror movies are outsiders as well, so that outsider syndrome reverberates within horror fans and geeky collectors. It's kind of a rallying call that brings fans and collectors together who are a little socially retarded, maybe.

Kirk Hammett

I'm world famous, everywhere I go there are people who love me because of I've been able to bring them some joy from the movies I've made.

Tony Curtis

I thought 'The Artist' was a perfect way to find a good balance. The artistic challenge is obvious because the film is black-and-white and its silent, but I did my best to make the movie accessible and easy to watch. I really don't want to make elitist movies. I really try hard to work for the audience. Audiences are smart. They get everything.

Michel Hazanavicius

I love the irony of movies. I really do. For whatever

reason, I'm incredibly intrigued by the irony of reality in a motion picture.

Zack Snyder

I can't do the same movies all my life. I'm conscious of that. But it's a trade-off. 'Dear John' allowed me to do movies I've wanted to do. You learn to balance it out. I'm still learning. Only now am I getting to do the kinds of movies that I have wanted to do. So it's a steady climb. You don't jump into a Soderbergh film.

Channing Tatum

I've been on so many movies. Generally, I haven't gotten to be on the ground level. As of two years ago, in 'Dear John,' I got to really be on the ground floor. I wasn't a producer. I felt like I put the work in, and I did have a lot of sway on what got fixed, reshoots, so on and so forth. It felt really good.

Channing Tatum

How many actors have a shot at being a part of something that became a part of pop culture? It's been very rewarding. I'm not getting the 20 million bucks for the new movies, but at least I'm getting warmth and recognition from people wherever I go.

Adam West

And there have certainly been movies I wanted to be in and milestones I wanted to surpass that did not happen.

Thomas Haden Church

Some of my favorite movies are action movies. You want something good to say. That comes from good writing. But writing is not a skill I possess, unfortunately.

Jason Statham

Being sensitive to the problem of women is just another symptom of the quality of movies: I don't think you can do anything that's very sensitive. Everything's sort of broad strokes and big gestures - adventure things that boys, guys want to see.

Teri Garr

I loved movies, but I can't remember ever really wanting to be an actress, and I certainly didn't imagine ever being in a movie. I think I wanted to be a writer.

Winona Ryder

I was always a fan of the old-style comics. I loved vaudeville. I loved Milton Berle, Dick Shawn, Phyllis Diller, Don Rickles, Charlie Callas, all those guys. Hilarious. I love the Bing Crosby and Bob Hope movies, and Abbott & Costello. My television influences were 'Monty Python's Flying Circus,' 'Benny Hill,' and 'Hee Haw.'

Larry the Cable Guy

The Jetsons had them in the 1960s. They were the defining element of 'Knight Rider' in the 1980s: cars that drive themselves. Self-driving cars appear in countless science fiction movies. By Hollywood standards, they are so normal we don't even notice them. But in real life, they still don't exist. What if you could buy one today?

Sebastian Thrun

All the movies where I play nice guys don't seem to do very well.

Claire McCaskill

As far as movies, I love 'The Notebook.' I always say that I wish I could play Rachel McAdams' character. She's amazing. That's the movie every girl wants to be in.

Miranda Cosgrove

When I was in seventh grade, I asked my parents for a mobile recording system for Christmas, and I got it. I didn't come out of my room for years after that. I'd get invited to the movies and I'd say, 'I'm gonna finish a couple of demos.'

Hunter Hayes

I used this line to demonstrate how important colors are in movies: It's not a caprice.

Pedro Almodovar

Critics can be harsh and I think it's going to take me a long time to make people see what I have inside of me and that I really put my guts into movies and that I'm not superficial and that I'm not just a pretty face.

Diane Kruger

I really care about this stuff, I care about movies, and you just have to be strong and don't be stupid; freedom of choice is a big responsibility, and I'm lucky enough not to have to just take any movie to pay the rent, so there's no need to be greedy.

Jonah Hill

I love it, man; I'm 23 years old and I'm lucky enough to write movies as a job! I just feel really blessed and can't believe it's happening.

Jonah Hill

I love animals and I love to see movies with animals that are done respectfully, you know?

Kristin Davis

I coach my daughter's softball and basketball team. We go to all the school functions. We go out to eat at night and take the kids to the movies. We try to be as normal as we can.

Tim McGraw

I once had a friend who did the hair for sci-fi movies, and after a particularly bad break-up I stupidly went to her salon and told her she could do anything she liked. She dyed the bottom cherry red and the top peroxide blonde.

Sally Phillips

It's all about escapism. That's essentially what all movies

are about. It's a vicarious thrill.

Todd Phillips

Now I'm seen by more people in one episode than I was in 20 years of theatre and movies. It's gratifying to have an impact on 25 million people a night, but I can say goodbye to my lunch-pail life as a working actor. I'm scared I might be a celebrity.

William Petersen

Luckily, I think, I never really wanted to be famous, I just wanted to make movies.

Seth Rogen

I'm not looking to lose anything. I'm looking to continue making movies.

Johnny Knoxville

We don't make movies for critics. I've done four movies; there's millions upon millions upon millions of people who've paid to see them. Somebody likes them. My greatest joy is to sit anonymously in a dark theater and watch it with an audience, a paying audience.

Michael Bay

Every time you have a carrot instead of a cookie, every time you go to the gym instead of going to the movies, that's a costly investment in your health. But how much you want to invest is going to depend on how much longer you expect to live in the future, even if you don't make those investments.

Emily Oster

Bill Hanna and I owe an awful lot to television, but we both got our start and built the first phase of our partnership in the movies.

Joseph Barbera

I'm not saying I'm a writer, but I've been in movies for a long time, and I think I could write a script for a movie.

Benicio Del Toro

I like to think of myself as a fairly educated human being, but I'm a very uneducated actor when it comes to movies, directors, producers, actors for that matter.

Shailene Woodley

I don't see my movies. I think it's healthier and safer to keep a bit of distance. I'm afraid to be disappointed.

Bernardo Bertolucci

I think that I used to love Hollywood movies. I remember great phases and moments. But, unfortunately, now is not the moment.

Bernardo Bertolucci

Whether or not we communicate it, I definitely seek my mom's acceptance and approval for everything. She has a strong commercial sense of movies and is a quintessential audience. When she doesn't like something, I know there is reason to worry. When she loves something, there is reason to celebrate.

Karan Johar

Oh I love horror movies, yeah. I think my favorite movie growing up was 'The Omen.' I actually wanted to be that little kid.

Norman Reedus

I don't care about movies. I tend to play badminton once a week.

Edward Witten

I always loved watching movies because I loved what certain moments inside of films did to me.

Jason Silva

I don't know if there is anyone who wouldn't want to play some kind of superhero. I don't know if the world is getting sick of superhero movies or not, but I think you will endlessly have actors who are intrigued by the idea of playing a superhero.

Jennifer Morrison

I'm quite comfortable looking at myself in movies, probably because I've been doing it for so long, since I was a kid. So I sort of watched myself grow up and go through adolescence, like, basically on camera.

Winona Ryder

People think that they just want movies like Pretty Woman, when really they - at least the ones that I know personally - have been waiting for something that doesn't completely insult them.

Winona Ryder

I don't care about my personal acting career anymore. I'm done with it. After 10 years of making movies and doing better than I ever could have imagined, I sort of had to ask myself: 'What am I supposed to do with all of this success that I have had?'

Kevin Spacey

Over a spell of about three years, I played a series of roles that were, for me, all very different, but most of them came out within a six-month period. They all dealt with a kind of dark territory that in some cases had been mined before in movies.

Kevin Spacey

I was very influenced by movies; I was very influenced by a world that had a sense of dream.

Ralph Lauren

It's like, if you can't focus on a movie for 90 minutes without looking at your phone, then don't go to the movies! You've got some issues, so you should probably stay home and work on those issues, and not distract everyone with lights, and sounds, oh my gosh, the tapping on the screens, it makes me crazy!

Ginnifer Goodwin

Take the hardcore gamers. The characters are way more real in the world of hardcore gamers who have played the game for hundreds of hours. They have the movie in their heads, they've built it on their own. These guys are always very disappointed in the movies.

Uwe Boll

They wanted me to do Scream 2, and I hate talking about movies I turned down, because it sounds judgmental. There's nothing wrong with horror movies. I enjoy watching them. The main reason I turn a part down is if I think I won't be good.

Casey Affleck

Part of the reason why movie bosses are so obsessed with crime movies is because they know that world and the criminals. And that's what they are - they would not hesitate to act illegally to achieve profit and gain.

Peter Mullan

I don't know what has happened to movies, but lately every movie is at least 20 minutes too long. It used to be that if you were three hours long it was because it was epic - a movie about Gandhi; something with very important subject matters.

Ethan Hawke

If you're not a real chameleon of an actor and if you're not one of those guys who can really shape-change themselves all the time, one of the ways to keep pushing yourself and keep changing is to be in different kinds of movies.

Ethan Hawke

I'm the number-one fan of gangster movies.

David Chase

I like the old, classic scary movies. I love 'Psycho,' 'The Sixth Sense,' and 'Poltergeist.'

Miranda Cosgrove

I'm not one of those actors where filmmakers that I admire ask me to be in their movies. I meet them at parties and they're nice to me, but they never ask me to work with them.

Seth Rogen

At the time I came along, Hollywood's idea of teen movies meant there had to be a lot of nudity, usually involving boys in pursuit of sex, and pretty gross overall. Either that or a horror movie. And the last thing Hollywood wanted in their teen movies was teenagers!

John Hughes

I heard about the movie business before I even knew what it was. So I surround myself now with people who are like, 'Can we not talk about movies for an hour?'

Jake Gyllenhaal

I should only have been as lucky as Valentino, in the movies - I didn't have to be a gigolo. In real life.

Cesar Romero

My best experiences with movies have come when I didn't know what to see.

Jean Paul Gaultier

I wish I could sit back and say, 'Oh, I'm gonna wait for a

Merchant-Ivory film to come my way. Or Ivory-Merchant. Whatever it's called. But you just take what's given and then, hopefully, down the road you can be more choosy and only do, say, Wayans brothers movies. That's my goal: to be more Merchant-Ivory-Wayans.

Zach Galifianakis

I grew up on the crime stuff. Spillane, Chandler, Jim Thompson, and noir movies like Fuller, Orson Welles, Fritz Lang. When I first showed up in New York to write comics back in the late 1970s, I came with a bunch of crime stories but everybody just wanted men in tights.

Frank Miller

From now on, I approach the cinema as a business woman. I intend to be in more action movies because, apart from Angelina Jolie, no other actress stands out in this genre.

Milla Jovovich

I used to love ninja movies. That was my thing.

Matt Smith

When you mutilate movies for mass media, you tamper with the hearts and minds of America.

Warren Beatty

I sort of have open invitations from a lot of people to do TV. But it's very hard for me to do roles in sitcoms and movies because I'm not a great actor, so if the material isn't good, I'm in torment while I do it.

Norm MacDonald

I think action movies bring more excitement than tears, but I always want to take it to another level. I mean, I think if one appreciates anything in life to a certain degree, it could possibly bring tears to your eyes.

Donnie Yen

Police/gangster films always have a huge following and huge audience because of the power, glamour, and certain fantasy aspect they have to them. When people watch movies, they like to fantasize being in a surreal world, and sometimes a criminal world can be attractive because you possess so much power and money, not like the average 9 to 5 guy.

Donnie Yen

Whether I'm acting or making it, at the end of the day it's telling the story; action, drama. You want the audience to feel it - the story, the action, the scene, or a particular shot. I just keep working on crafting my art, on how to make action movies.

Donnie Yen

I was the only swimmer in movies. Tarzan was long gone, and he couldn't have done them anyway; he could never have gotten into my bathing suit.

Esther Williams

I worked with Steven Spielberg on 'AI,' and his level of preparation was extraordinary. He told me there was a time at the beginning when he was a bit more spontaneous and went over budget, and it absolutely wrecked his head. When you look at the power and assuredness of his movies, it makes sense that he works out so much in advance.

Brendan Gleeson

I've seen little pieces of 'Interview with a Vampire' when it was on TV, but I kind of always go yuck! I don't watch R-rated movies, so that really cuts down on a lot of the horror.

Stephenie Meyer

For a number of years, I'd been around the kind of people who financed movies and the kind of people who are there to make the deals for movies. But I'd always had this naive idea that everybody wants to make movies as good as they can be, which is stupid.

David Fincher

I've never wanted to be the hottest star. I always wanted to do good movies.

Amanda Bynes

I am a theatre actor, but the last ten years I've taken parts in movies because it keeps me in money.

Michael Gambon

I always, always meant to be on stage. I only ended up even auditioning for television and movies because I was understudying a Turgenev play on Broadway and was so broke that, when I got a mini-series, I had to take it and was so ashamed because I was such a snob.

Jennifer Garner

But when you're writing a script - for me anyway - you have to sort of create an enforced innocence. You have to divest yourself of worrying about a lot of stuff like what movies are hot, what movies are not hot, what the budget of this movie might be.

David Cronenberg

I don't really want to do the Hollywood thing. I think you ought to try to say something with your movies.

Ellen Page

For years everyone looked toward the demise of radio when television came along. Before that, they thought talking movies might eliminate radio as well. But radio just keeps getting stronger.

Casey Kasem

You know, I put my little brother in the movies and he's still in the pictures. My mother makes me put him in the pictures.

Sam Raimi

There were very, very large sums of money that I made when I was very young - 15 million published works and a great many successful movies don't make nothin'.

L. Ron Hubbard

I've managed to do movies and still keep a lifestyle where I can go to ballgames, go to a grocery store like everybody else.

Chris Evans

For a lot of my childhood, I didn't want to direct movies because I didn't really know what directing was.

Peter Jackson

What I don't like are pompous, pretentious movies.

Peter Jackson

I can't stand modern movies. The images are too weird and eccentric for me.

Hayao Miyazaki

I've made 30 movies and for the most part my movies work. In a business where success is an exception and not the rule, I've mostly been successful.

Eddie Murphy

I adore watching movies; movie marathons are my favorite pastime. I can watch up to five movies back to back. I also love music and like reading whenever I get the time.

Priyanka Chopra

Paul Robeson was an athlete, Rutgers valedictorian, lawyer, writer, actor in movies and plays, great voice - a black male doing it all, back when some people thought he shouldn't. One reason I do all the things I do is to break stereotypes that people can only do certain things.

Dhani Jones

I think it's important that we have strong, female characters in movies now, which can really leave an impression on people - especially young people - and that they're not 'sexy' or 'cool.'

Saoirse Ronan

Meryl Streep's brilliant, just brilliant. I've been fortunate to do two movies with Meryl. And for an actor to go moment to moment like she does, there's no one better. And she dances between moments. Each take is different because she's riding instincts, she's riding impulses. And she trusts that.

Jeff Daniels

You know how I came up with the name 'Road to the Super Bowl?' It's an homage to the old Bob Hope - Bing Crosby buddy movies - you know, like 'Road to Zanzibar' or 'Road to Morocco.' Can you tell? All I've done my whole life is go to movies.

Steve Sabol

One of the great things about the 'Iron Man' franchise is that they employ fascinating actors who don't necessarily do action movies. Before 'Iron Man' you didn't associate Robert Downey, Jr. and Gwyneth Paltrow with those kinds of films. There's an emphasis on repartee and wit.

Rebecca Hall

I think we simply all like to project ourselves into somebody else - somebody who is better-looking, richer, smarter. It's comforting. It's escapism, and that, of course, is what the movies are supposed to be all about. Ultimately, I think it's just part of human nature to pretend.

Richard D. Zanuck

I made a decision back in 1978 that, in a trade off for money when I directed Halloween, I would have my name above the title in order to basically brand these movies my own.

John Carpenter

We think craft is important, and the irony has always been that horror may be disregarded by critics, but often they are the best-made movies you're going to find in terms of craft. You can't scare people if they see the seams.

James Wan

Honestly, I guess if you looked at my CV, I've been doing independent movies since I started. I think that I kind of took a few steps back from Hollywood as soon as it all started to come my way because I wasn't quite ready for the attention.

Josh Hartnett

There's nothing better than going to the movies and going into another world, and forgetting about everything that's happening outside.

Warwick Davis

I'm fanatical about movies: African, European, Viking, Roman. I got into witchcraft and magic from watching

'Bewitched' and 'The Wizard of Oz,' which shows in some of my outfits. I dress to reflect the whole spectrum of the universe.

Afrika Bambaataa

In the past, I had a knee-jerk approach to work, and it showed on screen. I was doing movies for the wrong reasons - trying to juggle dates, do too many guest appearances, take up projects under pressure or for emotional reasons.

Salman Khan

Cinema is entertainment, and people go to the movies because they want to feel good and forget about everything.

Vincent Cassel

While the notion that torture works has been glorified in television shows and movies, the simple truth is this: torture has never been an effective interrogation method.

Jerrold Nadler

Nothing was planned in my career. I just went with the flow and took everything that came to me. Selling potato chips was obvious, as it was a family business. When friends suggested I should try theatre, I gave it a shot. Then I did a lot of advertisements, and then movies happened.

Boman Irani

Why is the public so interested in movies about the wealthy? My answer is that Shakespeare wrote about kings. That's where the action is. And it's the classic, cathartic thing. You get to indulge in a lifestyle you're not part of, a tragic error leads to a downfall, and you get to say, 'Thank God I'm not him.'

Nicholas Jarecki

In anything I've ever written, all the characters sound like me, which I don't think is a bad thing. It makes sense. But I had always admired filmmakers who made movies that didn't sound like them at all.

Kevin Smith

I've wanted recognition; I wanted success; I wanted appreciation; I love the perks of being in the movies. I love the fame that comes with it - but that's why I became an actor.

Vidya Balan

I think I am too old to be doing teen movies. I am just kind of annoyed, because you have all these teen movies coming out with usually either Lindsay Lohan or Hilary Duff doing four of the exact teen movies over and over again.

Alexa Vega

I'm a big kid, I'm a kid at heart, so I still love the classic family films, such as the great Warner Bros film 'Willy Wonka and the Chocolate Factory' - not the remake, but the original. It's still one of the best movies, hands down, ever made, and of course that goes back to the ingenuity of the characters and the storyline.

Corey Feldman

Movies have these transcendent moments where everything is just right, from the dialogue to the music to the lighting to the narrative context; everything is just perfect, and something magical happens - the film breaks through the screen and does something to you.

Jason Silva

Among our many crimes as an imperialistic exploiter of other nations' cultures, stealing their movies ranks lower than selling them cigarettes but higher than killing their game. If you've seen big stupid American versions of

France's 'Three Men and a Cradle' or, recently, Japan's 'Shall We Dance?,' you can only mutter: 'Guilty, guilty, guilty.'

Stephen Hunter

With horror movies, a bigger budget is actually your enemy. You want to feel the rough edges, the handmade quality to good horror films. It's a genre that benefits from not having everything at your disposal.

Drew Goddard

On planes I always cry. Something about altitude, the lack of oxygen and the bad movies. I cried over a St. Bernard movie once on a plane. That was really embarrassing.

Michael Stipe

When Ginger Rogers danced with Astaire, it was the only time in the movies when you looked at the man, not the woman.

Gene Kelly

No, 'F/X 2' was a job. I enjoyed doing it but that was definitely a job. I wrote that, I didn't direct it but 'Candyman' and the earlier horror movies I made, I was completely into horror and suspense and always have been. It's informed everything I've done, even the way scenes are shot in 'Kinsey and 'Gods and Monsters.'

Bill Condon

Commercial movies have no feeling, no sensitivity. Most people tell me people won't understand films with feeling. But everyone can feel.

John Cassavetes

I don't want to compare myself to him - I don't want people to see me as this great genius - but when I see Charlie Chaplin's movies there is a combination of drama, naivety and social meaning that I can see in myself, at a different level.

Michel Gondry

I mean, movies are like your kids or your fingers and toes or something, it's pretty hard to pick favorites.

Sydney Pollack

'Little Miss Sunshine' snowballed. It was a tiny movie. We shot it in 30 days, and it was really fun to do, but it was one of those small movies that you don't hold out huge hope for.

Greg Kinnear

My husband and I are in preproduction of three movies, a Latin show, and a children's animation. I'm doing a very unique nail polish line, and finally, I'm developing a hair care line because people always ask me about my hair care system. I do a mask once a week that my grandma taught me how to make, so I want to share it with everyone.

Joyce Giraud

I don't like movies about serial killers, necessarily; it's too real and unpleasant for me.

Sam Raimi

I haven't done a lot of action movies, so it's kind of fun to get to do a lot of stunt work.

Mark-Paul Gosselaar

Some movies to me are like vampires - they suck all of the energy out of me and I don't like that. I like to give the audience energy if I can.

Sam Raimi

Whereas 'Avatar' and other movies get shocks out of their three-dimensionality, 'Gatsby' is going to be about inviting the audience into this larger-than-life drama, letting them almost be inside the room rather than looking at it through the window. I think it will really work.

Joel Edgerton

Obviously there's something very seductive about movies, which can be attractive in a bad way if you're doing them for the wrong reasons - for money, or for fame.

Andrew Garfield

I make movies that audiences like, that I'd want to see. That's all.

Michael Bay

I'm done with effects movies for now. When you do a movie like 'Transformers,' it can feel like you're doing three movies at once - which is tiring.

Michael Bay

I watch an awful lot of old Hollywood movies - I'll devour

anything with Bette Davis or Joan Crawford. My absolute favourite is 'Sunset Boulevard' starring Gloria Swanson.

Amanda Donohoe

Look, at the same time that I don't want to be a celebrity, I understand that when you make movies you put yourself out in the public eye. I'd be a baby and a fool to be like, 'Why are there cameras taking pictures of me?' when I'm on a billboard for a movie. I think that's a very absurd concept.

Jonah Hill

The comedy community is very friendly right now. I think that's why you see all the synergy and people doing each other's movies.

Jason Bateman

New forms of media - first movies, then television, talk radio and now the Internet - tend to challenge traditional codes of conduct. They flout convention, shake up the status quo and sometimes provoke outrage.

Willow Bay

I grew up with a lot of monster movies, robot movies,

since I was a kid. I love anime movies, like 'Evangelion' and 'Ghost in the Shell.'

Rinko Kikuchi

I watch mostly every martial arts movie... I really like movies that aren't just martial arts. I like movies that have spiritual meaning behind them, like samurai movies, or movies that have meditation.

Tony Jaa

Whenever I think about movies, I always look at that art process as having the best of a lot of worlds. Because if you watch a great film, you have a musical element to it, not just on the scoring, but in the way that the shots are edited - that has music and rhythm and time.

Frank Ocean

Some people go to the movies to be reminded that everything's okay. I don't make those kinds of movies.

David Fincher

When you make the kind of movies I make, you get weird letters from people.

David Fincher

I'm pretty upfront about my love and admiration for the military. One of the perks of making movies is that you get to sort of follow your own passions, and I believe quite passionately that we don't pay enough attention and respect to our veterans. Not just our wounded veterans, but all veterans.

Peter Berg

I would say the film world has stopped operating as one. We have divided it into Hindi movies, Bengali movies, Tamil movies and so on. Earlier, there was only one channel and we all knew what was going on. Today, it is hard to keep track of programmes due to the advent of regional channels.

Mithun Chakraborty

I so desperately hate to end these movies that the first thing I do when I'm done is write another one. Then I don't feel sad about having to leave and everybody going away.

John Hughes

Barbra Streisand is without a doubt one of the most honest people I have ever known. There is no doubt in my mind that she will not be doing any more concerts. Of course, she still will be making records and starring and directing in movies.

Marvin Hamlisch

'That's What She Said' is not Hollywood's standard picture of women: preternaturally gorgeous, wedding obsessed, boy crazy, fashion focused, sexed up 'girl' women. These are real women, comically portrayed, who are trying to wrestle with the very expectations of womanhood that Hollywood movies set up.

Carrie Preston

The way Hollywood portrays mothers - you're either all good and saint-like, or you're all bad. And I think the real honesty of motherhood is not given a voice in movies. I miss that as an audience member.

Ellen Barkin

I remember my first taste of American big movies was 'Ghost Rider.' I'm in two little scenes. But for those two little scenes they had 400 extras, upside-down stunt cars, and a fire brigade.

Rebel Wilson

Movies are a big part of our Indian culture.

Mahendra Singh Dhoni

All of my books have the potential to become movies, it's just a question of finding a studio who wants to get behind me and put up the money to make the movie.

Jackie Collins

I don't know any form of art or entertainment that can affect people the way movies can. I know it sounds ridiculous, but they can change your world. They can change your views.

Chris Evans

People just want to watch movies that are entertaining, it doesn't matter what genre it is.

Matthew Vaughn

It's hard to really get that excited about movies. Think about it like this: how many good comedy movies come out a year? Maybe one or two? And then, in those movies, what are the chances that there's a character that I'm the best fit to play? It's really small!

Aziz Ansari

I'm really visually stimulated more than anything. I don't really listen to music. I'm more into watching telly or watching movies and visual art.

Sia Furler

As a kid, I liked the 'Halloween' movies and 'Nightmare On Elm Street' and all that kind of stuff. But as an adult, I really don't watch much horror, to be honest.

Corey Feldman

I first heard African drum rhythms and chants at the movies. Then, when I had the opportunity to go to Africa and visit the villages, I heard the real, raw, true rhythms and realised the origins of the old Negro spirituals I grew up with in the South.

Isaac Hayes

There was a gap of seven years between the first and second Dracula movies. In the second one as everybody knows, I didn't speak, because I said I couldn't say the lines.

Christopher Lee

I started doing scary stuff when I was really little. I loved Halloween. It was a big holiday in our house, and my mother and I would start making our costumes back in July. So, it was a long process. And I always won the contest for the best, craziest costume. I would say I first came to horror through Halloween and then eventually through movies.

Jason Blum

The thing that is incredibly helpful is that we screen the movies and we ask the audience if they like it or not and we ask a lot of questions and do testing on the movies. For comedies, at least, it's very helpful. If they're not laughing and they don't say that they loved it, then I have screwed up.

Judd Apatow

During my school and college days, the three Khans - Aamir, Salman and Shah Rukh - were superstars for me and will always be. Their movies were eagerly awaited every Friday.

Shahid Kapoor

But, Tarantino has seen all of my movies. He's seen my

good stuff, he's seen my bad stuff, he's seen the ones I directed, he's read my autobiography. There's an awful lot of things he knows about me, all of which I think had something to do with his casting.

David Carradine

There's a lot of movies that aren't all about Christmas, or where Christmas isn't the focus, but have that spirit of Christmas in them. I love that sequence in 'Auntie Mame,' where she's in the department store, sewing at Macy's, and she doesn't know how to do anything but fill out a form as 'cash on delivery!'

Robert Osborne

For Sony, owning a studio is a gamble and probably a pretty good one, now that in the broadband era having content is a great advantage when you sell devices that in a ubiquitous world of distribution can actually show programs, movies, content directly to the consumer. So that you actually create, in a digital world, real synergy.

Howard Stringer

I love making movies, and being in any that I can be in. I'd like to be in those giant movies, as the fifth or sixth lead, and have three or four killer scenes. You don't have the responsibility of the entire movie being on you. I like those roles. I'm shooting for the middle.

Bill Burr

I wanted to do everything. I wanted to be a pilot. I wanted to be a secret agent. I wanted to be a fireman and a doctor, all that. So I related that through movies and stuff.

Josh Holloway

The perceived wisdom is that people do not go in large numbers to black-and-white movies anymore - which is a great shame, but I'd love to make a black-and-white movie one day.

Sam Mendes

I'm passionate about fantasy movies. I'm passionate about comic book movies. I'm passionate about superheroes. And movies about vengeance. And all of that - the stuff that I grew up reading.

Josh Keaton

My playing music is strictly for fun. When I was in a band, I was really excited to talk about it since I had never really played music to that extent. It was never meant as something I would consider as anything more than having fun with my friends. But I think I would enjoy writing music for the movies that I'm working on.

Anton Yelchin

Toward the end of school I started watching movies. Got a job in a movie theater in Brookline, Massachusetts.

Jim McKay

For me, horror movies are a real escape.

Lena Headey

The thing I find about the movie industry is that 99 percent of the people are absolute scum. They're horrible people, they really are. Very nasty killer rabbits who hate movies. But the other 1 percent are really the greatest, most wonderful people in the world.

Lloyd Kaufman

Well Ice H20 is my company that I plan to take to the next level with new artists, books, movies and so forth. It's more like a multimedia brand that I want to take to the next level and put some talented people on.

Raekwon

I hate Bollywood. The movies are all garbage, just terrible. It's my opinion; obviously, there are billions who like and love them. I don't like all the singing, dancing and all the dramatic crying. I have never seen a Bollywood film in my life.

Russell Peters

I don't believe in superheroes but I love Batman movies. There's a part of every person that is entertained by the idealistic, the fantastic.

Aisha Tyler

I can work every day of the year. TV is easy. My call's at 8:30 a.m. I'd like to break out of the comedy thing and take a shot at something serious like theater. The off-season allows me to do movies, but I'm not tired of TV yet. There's nothing like it. I've got the best of both worlds.

Scott Baio

When I'm feeling a little empty in the head, I like to go see movies or read to loosen things up there.

James Dashner

I had those kind of parents where I watched all of these very sophisticated movies: 'Five Easy Pieces', 'One Flew Over the Cuckoo's Nest.'

Sam Rockwell

I have my problems with 'Singles'. To me, 'Singles' is the least successful of the movies I've been lucky enough to make.

Cameron Crowe

When I produce a movie - and I've produced a number of movies, unlike Arnold - yes, I'm frustrated when the union says you can't do this, you can't work past that hour, you've got to break for lunch. But ultimately, they're right. What they do is for everyone's benefit.

Warren Beatty

Teen movies often have an unspoken underlying premise in which high school is seen as less serious than the adult world. But when your head is encased in that microcosm it's the most serious time of your life.

Rian Johnson

I've always wanted to be a Meryl Streep or a Natalie

Portman. I want to do all kinds of different movies, to be a chameleon. I don't want to limit myself.

Hayden Panettiere

The reason that I'm a writer today is because of Shakespeare and falling in love with Shakespeare when I was 8. That was through the movies, actually - through Olivier's 'Hamlet.' That was the first thing that got me to fall in love with Shakespeare and movies and everything in one big preadolescent rush.

John Logan

I've always been fascinated by Baretta and Donny Brasco, and other undercover cops in movies.

Dylan McDermott

I mean, movies are all geared to be basically under 25, and they're all tentpoles, explosions, excitement and all that - they take advantage of the big screen, which is great.

Joe Dante

I watched a lot of Douglas Fairbanks movies. He always played the same role with a mustache. Zorro had a mustache. The Musketeer had a mustache. Tarzan had a mustache.

Jean Dujardin

I want to continue to make beautiful movies. The most
important thing is to be a part of beautiful stories, that's all
I want. So I don't care if it's a Hollywood movie or an
independent movie or a Spanish or American movie. I care
about telling stories.

Melanie Laurent

I don't like gratuitous violence. I don't like the 'Saw'
movies. I don't like the 'Hostel' movies. I don't like
anything that is violence for violence's sake.

Michael Biehn

As a kid, I said, 'I want to write for movies.' When I finally
had that opportunity it was like I was able to exhale. 'Wow,
I'm finally doing this for real.'

Cliff Burton

I became a director just for the love of movies, because of
the power of cinema.

Antoine Fuqua

I was an absolute idiot, wearing polo-necks, reading Kerouac, watching Woody Allen movies, and jazz fitted right into all of that. My interest in that whole world became very genuine, but perhaps started off a bit affected - a mixture of right and wrong reasons. I was always drawn to non-commercial music, perhaps pathologically so.

Jamie Cullum

I did martial arts since I was 10 years old, and I've got as much love for the movies as I have for martial arts, so when I was 18 years old, I started studying performing arts with the eye of getting into the film industry and went to drama school after that.

Scott Adkins

I feel like every time I go out, I want to do a good job. I want people to say that he's just as good at stand-up as he is in some of the movies I've seen him in, so I try to do the best every time I go out there.

Chris Tucker

I want to keep working, I want to keep doing my humanitarian stuff around the world, shining light on different places that have problems. Keep making movies, make people laugh.

Chris Tucker

Making people laugh is giving, and it's healing, too, when people can go up to the movies and forget about their problems. It's a good thing. That's why I want to work.

Chris Tucker

God didn't make me to make movies, flex muscles, buy gold. What you love the most becomes your God... If I never make another dollar, my life is complete.

Mr. T

I love doing big movies. It's awesome! You have all these toys. The thing I like about this movie is, like they always say, directors have the biggest train sets! Don't tell anyone, but I'd do this for free.

Michael Bay

It goes all the way back to 'Psycho.' Movies with twists like that are memorable because they're so simple.

Steve Zahn

There are some movies I can watch over and over, never get sick of. I'll put one of those on and be puttering around the house. Then a certain scene will come on and I'll just have to go over and watch.

David Fincher

I spend way too much time watching television, going to sports games, going to movies. It struck me that there's an awful lot of data in the public domain for these sectors. The movie industry publishes weekly sales numbers - not many industries do.

Anita Elberse

It's a cliche, but Americans are puritanical. In their movies, they are scared of sex, but they overindulge in violence. I could have cut a G-rated version of 'Y Tu Mama Tambien' that would have pleased the American ratings board, but it would have been five minutes long.

Alfonso Cuaron

It's seldom that you find great moments in television. Usually you remember - in 'Breaking Bad' or any of these other great shows - you remember situations or characters. Not moments. But I have to say, I can make the same argument for mainstream movies, which have bad narratives and also no memorable moments.

Alfonso Cuaron

'Y Tu Mama Tambien' is one of the first unrated movies to be nominated for an Academy Award for Best Original Screenplay. But many video stores won't take a movie that's not rated, so I had to make the movie an R.

Alfonso Cuaron

In a sense I feel very much a part of the cinema now in a way where when I come back to the theater now I feel like a visitor. The cinema is really what I enjoy. I want to do more independent movies.

Brian Cox

The hardest thing to do in movies is be a day-part player. You have to go in, make your mark, and get out. There's a lot of leading actors who are not good for a lot of a movie, and then suddenly they have good moments, and they're like stepping-stones across a particularly feisty stream. They build careers out of that.

Brian Cox

I'm trying to become a young CEO, to brand myself in television and movies.

Bow Wow

I haven't seen Clones, which has been during this period when I haven't seen much of anything, but I did see Phantom Menace, and see my feelings about it - see, first of all, I think that when you make a lot of movies, your attitude about the movies changes.

Lawrence Kasdan

We grew up as kids watching those movies and we were exposed to themes of civil rights, unfairness, bigotry and fathers struggling against the kind of mob of the town, so you remember how you felt as a kid being taken seriously, that you are part of the human drama.

Rachel Griffiths

You never know when you read a script how it's going to turn out because so much depends on the collaboration between people. If I'd been in some of the movies I turned down, maybe they wouldn't have been a success.

Molly Ringwald

I've been making the best movies at Elegant Angel since Tom Byron left.

Marc Wallice

Whether it is the cavemen in the caves thousands of years ago, Shakespeare plays, television, movies and books, stories and characters take us on a journey. All I do is tell those stories without scripts and without actors.

Mark Burnett

I got into the movies by accident. When I got an offer, I thought, 'Let's try this, too.' Everything in my life has happened by trial and error. I didn't even think I would win the Miss India title, so where's the question of thinking I'd come this far.

Priyanka Chopra

I don't make crappy movies. I spend two or three years making a film. I don't take myself seriously, but I take my movies very seriously.

Lloyd Kaufman

I wouldn't say no to becoming a Bond girl. Making it in Hollywood has been my dream ever since I was little, watching Marilyn Monroe movies. To star in a Bond movie would be bliss on a stick.

Laura Haddock

My movies are not movies of answers but of questions.

Alejandro Amenabar

You know, I started doing movies. I mean, my mind was brought into saying, 'You know what? I want to build a generation of wealth.'

Master P

Ideally I'd like to be working steadily as an actor: movies, a TV series, that sort of thing. I've been through a few different TV development cycles, and they didn't work out. When the time and project are right, it'll come together. Like I tell a lot of guys, it's not a race; there's no finish line.

Russell Peters

It wasn't until I saw James Dean that I began to think that maybe I could actually do this. Movies didn't have to be just this fantasy with this impossibly handsome guy.

Terence Stamp

All my cousins are almost old enough to start seeing my movies. I'm going to have some 'splainin' to do.

Evan Goldberg

I remember the first time Bill Fichtner and I had a scene together. I've seen him in a few movies, from 'Armageddon' to 'The Perfect Storm' and 'Contact,' and suddenly he's on a bunk bed and I'm on a bunk bed and we're doing this scene together. That was a real 'pinch me' moment.

Chris Vance

I dream of working with iconic directors such as Tim Burton, Baz Luhrmann, Terry Gilliam and Wes Anderson - so I'm setting my sights pretty high! My perfect role would be in a fairy-tale period piece, and I'm quite upset all the Harry Potter movies have been made as I'd love to have been in those.

Dree Hemingway

George Raft may or may not have gone both ways, but he was very sensitive to what they said about him, and it was one factor why he decided to play all those gangsters in the movies.

Cesar Romero

I now, more and more, appreciate when I'm in a group of good people and get to work in good movies and projects. I'm wildly grateful and appreciative.

Jeff Goldblum

I've started movies without screenplays both on 'Clash' and on 'Hulk,' and that is tremendously stressful because you have a tendency to overcompensate with effects. You haven't tested it in your head. You didn't run it over and over again and covered all of the plot holes and figure it out. It's a marathon that you sprint.

Louis Leterrier

I like to go out, but sometimes it's nice to stay cozy at home, watching movies or TV, especially early in the week.

Charlotte Ronson

Yeah, I do like scary movies, especially the ones that don't take themselves too seriously.

Anna Faris

We were a Western civilisation, an English speaking civilisation, both NZ and Australia, and we had all these influences coming from both Great Britain and America to us; sending us their culture in the shape and form of movies and television.

Richard O'Brien

I grew up loving monsters. I'm just a total monster geek. When I was a kid, I had the Aurora monster models, and I would make them. I loved the Universal horror movies and the Hammer movies. I just had an affinity for them.

John Logan

I've love to do more movies. Just because I'm interested in the medium very much. I've done a lot of theatre at this point, and I've done a lot of TV. I've done a few independent films, but a lot of them have not seen the light of day. It'd be really nice to be in a film that gets out there.

Morena Baccarin

I've always been a huge fan of the 'Pirates of the Caribbean' movies.

Abigail Breslin

I grew up on the Bond movies. The first one I saw was 'Diamonds Are Forever,' when I was a kid. I just loved them to pieces.

John Logan

The only time I ever met a character that I wrote was when I met Ian McKellan, when he was playing Magneto in the 'X-Men' movies.

Grant Morrison

I don't actually watch many shows. I will either watch movies or football. I enjoy to watch games in the Premier League and will also watch movies a lot as well. That is how I relax.

Xavi

I think everybody has something that takes them away or makes them happier. To some people it's baseball or sports or knitting or the movies.

Sutton Foster

I never play a villain that I don't have something I can either do or say so the audience sees there is something redeemable about them. In other words, I don't want to do evil for evil's sake. I don't want to do Jason slasher movies. There's no point in that.

Brion James

I think most people, even if they say they hate horror movies, there's that feeling you get inside that you love. I mean, I love it. I love to have the hairs on the back of my neck stand up or get that chill up my spine.

Barry Watson

Actually, I look the same in real life as I do in the movies.

Andy Lau

I've done movies that I've been advised not to do. 'Dog Soldiers,' the movie I did 11 years ago now, I remember my agent at the time was like, 'You shouldn't do that. It's a weird film about werewolves,' and it became a cult hit.

Kevin McKidd

I still remember 1997 when I made the movie 'Storm Riders;' that moment, a lot of American producers want to hire me to make movies in the States.

Andrew Lau

The power of the human spirit inspires me. Movies, books, stories, people, anything that reminds us that we are more than just this physical body and our capacity for love and courage can bend reality.

Caity Lotz

I don't like to go to the movies to see violence or some kind of spy thing with all kinds of information you have to assimilate to understand the plot.

Pia Zadora

I grew up in Los Angeles, and I've made movies all over the world... I've been in New York, Norway, Chicago, Pittsburgh, Philadelphia, London - I've been in all these cities, shooting away in the winter, thinking, 'People who choose to live here are insane.'

John Landis

For me, the sound design and the musical score is a big part of what makes scary movies work.

James Wan

I have terrible taste in things: music, movies, TV shows. I love all the guilty pleasures: Bravo, 'Real Housewives.'

Grace Helbig

When my friends and I would act out movies as kids, we'd play the guys' roles, since they had the most interesting things to do. Decades later, I can hardly believe my sons and daughter are seeing many of the same limited choices in current films.

Geena Davis

People don't know what they are doing most of the time. They don't know what they want. It's only in 'the movies' that they know what their problems are and have game plans to deal with them.

John Cassavetes

I'm not surprised that Spielberg was able to capture the heroism of Schindler; so many of his movies are about the better part of mankind.

Gene Siskel

Now, being on the cover of Vanity Fair is as important as being in great movies. The lines are very, very blurred.

Jason Patric

There are many movies that have done it very badly. The studios have gone for quick profits and audiences are feeling angry. People aren't taking the time and spending the money to do it right. I am.

Michael Bay

I don't take acting classes - I'm quite an autodidact. I prefer to learn from other actors by watching various movies. Evaluate my acting, spot the flaws and fix them.

Joe Taslim

I want to do movies, television and theater. Whatever comes along.

Ansel Elgort

When I did a study of all the coming-of-age movies that meant a lot to me, whether it was 'The Graduate' or 'Rebel Without a Cause' or 'Dead Poet's Society,' they all had that timeless feel. None of them were completely married to the details of their age. They felt timeless in their treatment of it. That's what made them resonate with me.

Stephen Chbosky

I'm horrible at quoting movies! Even my very favorites are not easily recalled or programmed to memory. When people start movie quoting around me, I'm that person who just smiles and then looks up the reference later.

Ashley Rickards

I just got an iPhone, which is cool, but I don't download movies, I don't watch Hulu, I don't have Netflix. I don't do any of that. But I do geek out to music.

Miles Teller

I've always loved music. I listen to music the way a lot of actors watch movies.

Penn Badgley

The most difficult part of making movies is to keep making them. Maybe, you could make the biggest hit in the world, but then the big problem is what to do next and how to maintain devoted to a certain instinct that I have about films.

Emir Kusturica

I used to just daydream all the time about being in movies, from the age of, like, four onwards. I would sit down and watch movies with my father and my grandfather, and always pretended that I was in the stories.

Aneurin Barnard

This is what I always wanted to do in my entire life, so I am not going to sit here and complain that it is so terrible to be in successful movies, because it becomes a trilogy!

Alyson Hannigan

I thought Clint Eastwood was cool in all the western movies, but I'm not gonna drive somewhere he's at and stand in line to see him. I told Missy, my wife, 'The only person I'd stand in line for is God Almighty. You made the universe? All right, I'll get in line!'

Jase Robertson

I think it's sad that movies and television have caused the theatre to fade as a popular art form. I hope to get young people into the theatre and expose them to Shakespeare.

Kelly McGillis

There's been about 75 movies about Jesse James, and I've seen about four of them. He's usually portrayed as this plucky rebel who's got no choice but to turn to crime, because the railway's hassling his mother. But he wasn't like that.

Andrew Dominik

My favourite actors are all dead or dying. I just love Jimmy Stewart, Bette Davis, Katharine Hepburn - I was named after her - and Cary Grant. I just love old black and white movies and the stars in them. It must have been a great time to be in Hollywood.

Katharine Isabelle

I don't know what is in store for the movie business any better than anybody else does, but it does seem like my kind of movies are a little trickier than it used to be - or maybe a lot trickier.

Wes Anderson

I've never had a movie that got great reviews. I've had movies that got different levels of good and bad reviews, but you can more or less count on plenty of bad reviews.

Wes Anderson

It's only in relatively recent years that Hollywood became the playground of multinational corporations which regard movies and TV shows as a minor irritant to their overall activity.

Peter Bart

I'm kind of a homebody. I like to sit at home and watch movies and eat good food.

Emilie de Ravin

I would love to do comedy. I think I'm funny and that comedy is my strong suit, at least in real life. I have yet to prove myself in the movies, but I'd love to get the opportunity to do that.

Evan Peters

In the future, I kind of like the idea of doing music for film. I think that would be a nice job. I've always liked the sound aspect in movies. I guess once I have more instruments under my belt, it could be something I could do.

Christopher Abbott

The vampire movies I embraced as a kid used vampirism as a metaphor that expressed deep sadness and a lot of human qualities.

Alexandra Cassavetes

I was familiar with that and 'Rio Bravo.' 'Rio Bravo' was what John Carpenter did, that brilliant move of taking a western and turning it into an urban flick. And from there you got, you know, all the cop genre movies of the time.

John Leguizamo

You may have seen me in movies like 'Fast & Furious' and 'Avatar.' But I wouldn't have been able to do any of that without hard work and determination. You can accomplish anything if you just stay out of trouble and do the right things.

Laz Alonso

Movies either work or they don't work and they're either funny or they're not and we work very hard. To achieve that kind of work is really kind of delicate stitching.

Ivan Reitman

With all due respect to the people who made the motorcycle movies during the '60s, I felt the sophistication level could be a bit higher, and I felt I could raise the bar on that, too.

Larry Bishop

I spend a lot of time at my son's school and I really wanted to do a movie that the kids could see. The good thing about being my age and not having to be the ingenue anymore is that I get to be a mom. I get to have kids in my movies.

Virginia Madsen

Summer movies are spectacles; that's what you pay 10 dollars to see. You want to get teased by effects sometimes. I think that will never stop.

Jan de Bont

Write comic books if you love comic books so much that you want to write them. Don't write them like movies. Comics can do a lot of things that movies can't do, and vice versa.

Grant Morrison

I think people would be most surprised to know that I love

scary movies.

Olivia Holt

I want to have some effect on the way the world works in whatever way I can, and I also want to have the power to help get the movies that I think are important made.

Maggie Gyllenhaal

I live, therefore I make films. I make film, therefore I live. Life. Movement. I make home movies, therefore I live. I live, therefore I make home movies.

Jonas Mekas

I miss the movies. Still, I understood that my kind of movie has had its day. I thought it was over for me.

Debbie Reynolds

Even the shows or movies that we know are not going to change the world, I love this. I love 'em. I'm a movie fan. I'm a nerd of any kind. I love a big studio comedy as much as I love the teeniest tiniest of indie. I'm not a snob in that way. I really do like a big, big studio comedy.

Kathryn Hahn

I can no more reread my own books than I can watch old home movies or look at snapshots of myself as a child. I wind up sitting on the floor, paralyzed by grief and nostalgia.

Francine Prose

One of my favorite movies of all time is 'It's A Wonderful Life,' which is a pretty interesting choice for a seasonal Christmas favorite, because it's about a guy who wants to commit suicide and is presented with reasons not to.

Frank Darabont

While I'd like to make movies that are uplifting, there's always that part of you that goes, 'I want to play the evil guy because it's not me.' So anything that is not me is a challenge, and if I rise to the challenge, then I've kind of proved myself.

Dean O'Gorman

It seems when I put together records, as Henley used to say, they're just like movies. They should have action, tension, love scenes, places to relax.

Glenn Frey

Just to get a job is always really exciting to me. I do feel there's a lot left for me to learn about movies, the subtleties of acting.

Sebastian Stan

I call 'Community' the best day job in the world, because between takes, I get to write music. I get to write sketches. I get to write movies. It's the best job ever.

Donald Glover

The history of horror movies goes back a long way... of people trying to convincingly be terrified when looking at a piece of tape on the side of the camera box. I have a whole new respect for it.

Josh Hamilton

I am actually really boring and I lead a quiet life. I love being at home, cooking for my boys, watching movies and I like nothing better than to go to bed early with a book.

Patsy Kensit

I think the best part in going to the movies is you feel

something and you relate whether it's to family struggles or dimming your light for someone. I would say to never dim your light and to really, truly follow your dreams.

Tika Sumpter

When I watch movies or TV, I am like, 'Wow that guy is really cute, I really like him,' but I don't really have one person that I would die to go to something with. There are so many hot guys.

Sasha Pieterse

I love movies, but I think people think relationships are supposed to go how they go in movies. The ones I like are the ones that represent life.

Cristin Milioti

Unless you're a big movie star, regular television work is going to bring you more exposure than anything. Everybody has a television; not everybody goes to the movies.

G. W. Bailey

I have a maple leaf tattoo over my heart, quite literally, and my two favorite things on Earth are being in Canada and making movies.

Jay Baruchel

I found, through the process of doing 'The Perks of Being a Wallflower,' that I really love directing movies and I love writing books and so this will become the centerpiece of my career for the next ten or twenty years. Doing these adaptations.

Stephen Chbosky

When young people see movies like 'Gandhi 'or 'JFK,' there is an element of romanticization of these powerful people, and young people often feel a huge distance between their own lives and the lives of these social-change heroes. But the Panthers were flawed-up people from the streets, so it's easier to identify with them.

Mario Van Peebles

I came to Southbury because I wanted to live a more simple life. When I was a child, I saw lots of movies about happy people living in Connecticut. And ever since then, that was where I wanted to live. I thought it would be like the movies. And it really is. It's exactly what I hoped it would be.

Polly Bergen

For me, there was no great myth around the movies when I was a young child. My father was very simple about the whole thing. He did not consider cinema an art. Cinema was entertainment. Literature and music were art.

Jacques Audiard

I always wanted to play a boxer because some of my favorite films, as a boy, were those great boxing movies, like 'Raging Bull', 'Rocky', 'The Set Up', 'Fat City and Hard Times'. I just loved those films.

Holt McCallany

But he did say that the character would be on the sidelines in movies One and Two, and move into the middle with number Three, but I didn't realize he would move in with quite such a bang.

Ian McDiarmid

I think a great first date would be something different... not like movies or going to dinner... going rock climbing together... doing an activity and then going to dinner, so that you guys share an experience, and then you have something to talk about, and it's not the same old thing.

Madeline Zima

We watch so many TV shows and movies about jaded or corrupt policemen, we forget people join the police force to do good, and they really care about that.

Enrico Colantoni

Whether as victim, demon, or hero, the industrial worker of the past century filled the public imagination in books, movies, news stories, and even popular songs, putting a grimy human face on capitalism while dramatizing the social changes and conflicts it brought.

George Packer

Everyone loves the seventies because that's when movies were character-based, and you saw great characters and you saw very interesting filmmaking. There are interesting movies being made now, but it's harder and harder to make them.

Justin Bartha

I decided to be an actress, and the day after, I was an actress. That was quick and very scary at the same time. When 'Obscure Object of Desire' came out in France, I felt guilty for my friends at the National School who weren't in the movies. The whole thing was turmoil.

Carole Bouquet

My characters always start well in movies. Almost every movie I've done starts with a happy marriage, it's all beautiful, wealthy, whatever... and then of course my husband leaves me, and everything falls apart.

Carole Bouquet

As an actor I'm part of a long line of character people you can take back to the silent movies. There's always the little guy who's the sidekick to the tall, good-looking guy who gets the girl.

Curtis Armstrong

Rave music sounds like an electronic disco version of '30s Universal monster movies.

Mojo Nixon

Being non-commercial is never an ambition. Movies come together at different points for fortuitous reasons. You do them as you get the opportunity, as opposed to doing them when you choose to or design to.

Ethan Coen

The entertainment world, television, movies, social media, YouTube stuff, we're so bombarded with so much imagery and such a great sense of inhumanity, and there is a coarseness, a coarsening of interaction.

Steven Bochco

When you work on big commercial movies, of course there's more money involved and you can still do some good work. But with an independent, you get films that are really close to the writers' and directors' heart. Somehow it becomes a little deeper. A little more meat and not as much flash.

Dennis Haysbert

In San Paulo I went to the movies and by the time I left the theater there was a mob at the exit. I had never been in that kind of situation when we weren't on tour and there was a whole bunch of security. I'm a little dude, and out of nowhere to have 50 or 60 people come running towards me when I'm jut with my friend, it was kind of scary.

Kevin McHale

What career? A man's got a body of film of about four movies in about 10 years or something. I do it because I think I can do a good job of something and I'll enjoy it, do it, and sort of vanish. I don't want to be an actor for hire.

Paul Hogan

I think a lot of African-American kids don't have fathers to teach them how to dress, so you end up being taught by pictures in magazine and movies. You see cowboys, Indians, old Hollywood films, Cary Grant. It has an effect on you.

Andre Benjamin

During a movie, you lose all ability to focus on your own interests. Your life is in service. After that you just want to disappear, switch off the phone, and sleep and watch movies for a month.

Robert Richardson

When you look at movies, the lead girl is always gorgeous and thin. There is a stereotype that you need to look a certain way and when you get in the business you really feel the pressure.

Margot Robbie

I'm a huge, huge comic book fan. I love the superhero

movies so much. If I had to be one of the Avengers, I would go with Thor. I would have to. I just think I look the part too much, and I'm a fan of all of them, but Thor would be something that I think I could put on. I think I could make it happen.

Derek Theler

Christmas movies, it's a hard thing to do. The danger is you just end up with a Hollywood star with a Santa beard. You risk it being fake and cheesy and not real.

Peter Baynham

There are movies that I love tonally, that I would love to emulate. Anything from Wes Anderson or the Coen brothers is right in my wheelhouse, as something that I would aspire to. I love that kind of indie, fun, colorful, funny, sweet, heartfelt but dark film.

Sam Huntington

Making movies is eating candy. It's a very expensive candy, so you value when you can do it. So when you can do it twice at once, it's like, you know, a kid in a candy store!

Phillip Noyce

You can't think about how people will perceive you or your character. All you can do is focus on your work. The rest is up to the universe. I've been acting for 16 years. I've done 55 movies and, in all seriousness, there's maybe five that are good and the rest are crap.

Robert Patrick

I've done movies that were maybe not worth it, but I try to take the best from every experience. You learn more from bad experiences sometimes. It gives you more will to overcome your mistakes. They give you determination.

Violante Placido

I do like the zombie movies quite a bit. I know there are purist zombie guys that don't like the running zombies, but I dig the infected thing. I think that's a scarier incorporation of an element into the genre.

Mark Pellegrino

I think you have a responsibility to the people you're making movies with, and I take that very seriously. I don't want to let up and I don't want to let down.

Scott Rudin

If only I could step back into the time of old movies, if only I could be given the opportunity to do what Katharine Hepburn did or what Rosalind Russell did. Those kinds of characters, that kind of patter, that kind of language, that kind of script. They don't exist any more.

Kari Matchett

Making movies was a real weird kind of adult experience. In a way it was like MIT, in that it was a great education. The big lesson is, people are people. They're smart, funny, creative people, but they're people.

Charlie Korsmo

People think it must be wonderful being in movies or on television, but it can be very tough on a child. I had two friends in elementary school. That was it. There was a clique of girls that were brutal to me. They pulled some very mean stuff. My two friends got me through it. Without them, I would have been all alone.

Angela Cartwright

I grew up watching movies and television, and one day when I was really young I told my mom I wanted to become an actor, and she was really supportive and got me involved in local theater and commercials. From there I moved up to auditioning for movies and television.

Cameron Monaghan

Child actors come off as work being their life and doing it 24/7, but I still have those days where it's totally, like, whatever: shopping, movies, adventures.

Hailee Steinfeld

I love going to movies by myself.

Tyler Hoechlin

Old film-noir movies. There's something comforting about watching black-and-white movies, and hearing this kind of music just puts me in a fantasy world. It's a really great escape for me.

Petra Haden

I've done a lot of movies, but my favorite was 'Blind Faith.'

Courtney B. Vance

I spend days on my Xperia logging on Facebook chatting with my friends and family at home; I love listening to Rihanna and Pink and watching movies. Basically, anything that makes me smile, but most of my fans will know that I am always smiling!

Dominika Cibulkova

Movies are more than a commodity. Movies are to our civilization what dreams and ideals are to individual lives: They express the mystery and help define the nature of who we are and what we are becoming.

Frank Pierson

I don't think I could compare myself to Macaulay Culkin, because we're pretty much two different kinds of actors. He's done a lot of comedy. He does mostly just comedy like 'Uncle Buck' and 'Home Alone' and 'Home Alone 2.' And I've done a lot of different stuff, like sad movies, like the movie about the kid with AIDS.

Brian Bonsall

I tend to think of action movies as exuberant morality plays in which good triumphs over evil.

Sylvester Stallone

When I felt like an outsider, movies made me feel inside my own skill set.

Steven Spielberg

As a writer, one of the things we all learned from the movies was a kind of compression that didn't exist before people were used to watching films. For instance, if you wanted to write a flashback in a novel, you once had to really contextualize it a lot, to set it up. Now, readers know exactly what you're doing. Close-ups, too.

Salman Rushdie

I like fantasy. I like horror, science fiction because I can get avant-garde with those performances in those movies.

Nicolas Cage

I have eclectic tastes in the movies I want to do.

Nicolas Cage

I do enjoy animated movies.

Nicolas Cage

I'm told we movie critics praise movies that are long and boring.

Roger Ebert

I like movies that are scary, but I don't want them to be dirt dumb. I want a movie that gets my blood racing, makes me laugh, but also gives me something to think about, with maybe a little sexy thrown in. Hollywood doesn't make movies like that.

Penn Jillette

I realise how important it is to use the time I have. I respect people who want to do that by watching television. I happen to want to read books. But I know I can't read all the books or watch all the movies in one lifetime.

Viggo Mortensen

I had seen movies before that that had made me laugh, but I had never seen anything even remotely close to as funny as Richard Pryor was, just standing there talking.

Joe Rogan

Reality TV looks more like America than movies do.

Gabrielle Union

There's too much down time making movies. That leads to boredom. And that leads to trouble.

Jeremy Renner

I rarely see one of the 'summer blockbuster' movies. I'd like to see a stronger focus on smaller, smarter movies.

Christopher Meloni

A lot of actors get concerned about their own image, even going so far as to rewrite a movie to best serve that image. All I want to do is be in good movies.

Michael Douglas

All movies aren't fun; some are hard work. You try to do something and convey a set of emotions that have to do with some real life kind of stuff.

Samuel L. Jackson

When I go to movies I generally want to be taken to another world.

Darren Aronofsky

I have kind of a funny relationship with movies. I don't have to see the whole movie to get an impression of it or to let it have an influence on me.

Lana Del Rey

I'll tell you what I really enjoy. We all go to the movies, we all watch television, we know what they're about, how they work. When the main character is a cop or a spy, it's very exciting, but I also very much enjoy when the main characters are nobodies - a trucker.

Nathan Fillion

I think people like to see the lives of artists that are legends. They always go through the dark periods and I think just as humans we like to see that and them coming out of it. I love those kinds of movies.

Kristen Wiig

I've always been shy, but I see that as a good thing because it kept me focused on music. When I was in seventh grade, I asked my parents for a mobile recording system for Christmas, and I got it. I didn't come out of my room for years after that. I'd get invited to the movies and I'd say, 'I'm gonna finish a couple of demos.'

Hunter Hayes

Movies are the shadiest business in the world.

Jessica Alba

I can't really remember my life without movies.

Elle Fanning

Well, getting behind the camera is something I've always wanted to get involved with. Ever since I was doing movies like 'Zathura' I was very interested in all the different jobs on set and kind of soaking all the information up like a sponge.

Josh Hutcherson

I've kind of come to the conclusion that what passes for realism in movies has nothing to do with reality and that my stuff is more realistic than that.

Charlie Kaufman

I'd like to produce. I'd like to come up with ideas and collaborate with people and directors and writers that I like, be a part of movies that have the same idea that the movies that impacted me have. I'd like to be able to do that for people.

Emma Stone

Sometimes I make very selfish choices; like I did 'Once Upon A Time' for my inner 8-year-old and my hypothetical future child. I've done some movies because I would regret them if I didn't, but other projects I've done because they've scared me or if I felt I needed to do a big romantic comedy to help me professionally.

Ginnifer Goodwin

When we shoot 24, there are so many things I have to worry about, from the script to technical things to my performance, that I don't have a second to be bored or take anything for granted. We produce 24 hours of film a season, which is like making 12 movies.

Kiefer Sutherland

Besides writing music and surfing, I like to simply chill with my friends. Watching movies and going out to eat are often my prime choices for a day off.

James Maslow

I'm like, 'What world am I living in?' Aren't movies made

to have something to say? Why make a movie if you don't have something to say? What are you doing it for? Are you doing it because you want to make a lot of money?

Jake Gyllenhaal

My movies were the kind they show in prisons and airplanes, because nobody can leave.

Burt Reynolds

I didn't see Dr. No for a year, but I liked it when I saw it. It was a fun movie. I don't like the Bond movies now. I hate special effects.

Ursula Andress

I seem to have a knack for picking movies that go on to be cult favorites.

Kurt Russell

I'm a big 'Star Wars' fan and grew up watching the movies. I read all the books and have read 'Star Wars' fiction that went between the newest trilogy and the original trilogy and it was part of my childhood.

Jared Padalecki

I do love horror movies, but I'm not the kind of guy who would dress up as a ghoul for Halloween. I might go as a member of the Blue Man Group.

Christopher Mintz-Plasse

Work is good when people are responsible, and in low-budget movies a lot of the actors don't want to be there. They're there to build a resume.

Sean Young

It gets so boring at home. After all, how many reruns of Abbott and Costello movies can a guy watch on television?

Bud Abbott

I used to watch every episode of 'Justice League,' I went to all the movies, I had the Superman lunchbox. I was enamored with animation in general and always wanted to somehow be a part of it.

Jesse McCartney

A woman wants to be romanced. She wants to be an essential part of a great adventure; she wants a beauty to unveil. That is what little girls play at, and those are the movies women love and the stories that they love.

John Eldredge

So I got caught up in the same wave as everybody else and went right out to Hollywood, to make movies.

Kitty Carlisle

'Batman Begins' came out and it was really successful, and it had gritty naturalism. And suddenly... I can't tell you how many movies I was pitched where it was, 'We want to do what you did with 'Batman' but with 'Teenage Mutant Ninja Turtles," or whatever.

David S. Goyer

I love to just go to the movies, watch movies, listen to the scores and all that 'cause that's, like, the next step for me.

Akon

After the war, there was no industry. We lost the war. We had our whole city destroyed. No money. No studio. No film. No camera. No equipment. We would shoot in the street. We had no actors. Nothing. But we wanted to do movies. And we did the best movies in the world.

Dino De Laurentiis

If audiences are sort of interested in movies that are made like McDonald's hamburgers, which do have a value in the world, then we have to re-evaluate our entire career.

Lana Wachowski

Movies are written in sand: applauded today, forgotten tomorrow.

D. W. Griffith

My father loved 'Godard and Truffaut.' He was more artsy. My mom loved the 'Bourne' trilogy; she likes big blockbusters. She loved that I did 'I Am Legend.' My passion for acting came with my passion for movies.

Alice Braga

All these horror movies are slasher film now. I like them, they're fun, but they wink at the audience and you're really not terrified through the movie.

Gina Philips

Movies are all about plot. Theater, even if it's story heavy, it's about ideas.

Harvey Fierstein

Movies are all about plot. Theater, even if it's story heavy, it's about ideas. Theater has to resonate in your heart in a way that movies don't.

Harvey Fierstein

When I was a kid, I thought movies just came from air. I thought they just appeared.

Clint Eastwood

Movies are fun, but they are no cure for cancer.

Clint Eastwood